Inextinguishable Blaze

Inextinguishable Blaze

Meditations on
Charles Wesley's Hymns

Andrew Pratt

Copyright © Andrew Pratt 2007

Cover image copyright © PurestockX

British Library Cataloguing in Publication data
A catalogue record for this book is available
from the British Library

ISBN 978-1-905959-06-1

First published by Inspire
4 John Wesley Road
Werrington
Peterborough PE4 6ZP

Printed and bound in Great Britain by
Stanley L Hunt (Printers) Ltd
Rushden, Northants

Acknowledgements

Hymn texts have been taken, sometimes with amendment, from *HymnQuest 2006*, published for The Pratt Green Trust by Stainer & Bell Limited, PO Box 110, Victoria House, 23 Gruneisen Road, London N3 1DZ.

Scripture references are taken from the New Revised Standard Version of the Bible (Anglicized Edition) © 1989, 1995 by the Division of Christian Education of the National Council of the Churches of Christ in the United States of America. Used by permission. All rights reserved.

Some use has been made of:

The Works of John Wesley, A Collection of Hymns for the Use of the People Called Methodists, 8 vols, ed. by Franz Hildebrandt and Oliver A. Beckerlegge (Oxford, Clarendon Press, 1983), VII.

A History of the Methodist Church in Great Britain, Volume 1, ed. by Rupert Davies and Gordon Rupp (London, Epworth, 1965).

This book is dedicated to my wife, Jackie,
with whom I share a deep love of these hymns

Contents

Holy Week and Easter

The conversion of John and Charles Wesley

Pentecost

Trinity

The Body of Christ

Transfiguration

Summer days

Introduction

'Hark, the herald angels sing', 'Love divine, all loves excelling' – we all know them in spite of the fact that they were written over 200 years ago. Many people can sing these hymns by heart and so it's worth commemorating the birth of their author. He was Charles Wesley and 2007 is the 300th anniversary of his birth. He was born on 18 December 1707, the sixth of the seven Wesley children who ultimately survived childhood. His brother John was four years his elder. I hope that as people read through this book, the reflections will sometimes give an insight to the meaning of the hymns, or set them in a new light so that we can continue to value them.

I have enjoyed the process of reading these hymns again Sometimes just the act of reading instead of singing has brought the words to life. Invariably I have found that Charles Wesley's words continue to inspire me, and my faith has been strengthened as I have read familiar as well as forgotten texts. Being a hymn writer myself I have been humbled by Charles Wesley's ability to reflect on faith, interpret Scripture, to comfort or to challenge, to sow the seeds of hope. I am amazed that these words have been taken round the world, translated into different languages and sung to different settings in a continuous process of rediscovery. Part of their use today is in the way in which people not only sing them in church, but read them at home as part of their own prayers, in their own devotions.

The book contains 52 hymns set out in such a way that the reader can study one for each week of the year, beginning with Advent.

Most hymns fall into misuse within a hundred years or so. Those that don't often seem outdated and have lost their usefulness. So why produce a collection of hymns that are so old? In this case there are many reasons and not simply to mark an anniversary.

Much of what Charles Wesley wrote is good poetry and has been 'canonized' as such. Those who love this form of expression will happily read Alexander Pope or John Milton, William Wordsworth or Gerard Manley Hopkins. Wesley, at his best, could be ranked with any of these. He differs, it goes without saying, in having a wholly Christian output, but also because he wrote for growing Christian communities to help them to explore and remember their faith. All his verse is religious and he has been marginalized by secular critics because of this. If such prejudice is put aside, however, we find poetry of an unusually consistent quality, given the vast amount that he wrote. So the words are worth preserving for the poetry alone.

It is fashionable to be rational in our understanding of the world and our interpretation of experience. In this way, we tend to avoid anything that is not concrete, that cannot be verified or scientifically tested. Everything is earthbound. Now there is good reason for this. I'd rather be operated on by a surgeon who knows about anatomy than one who claims no knowledge. I'd rather fly in a plane put together in accordance with engineering principles than one based on poetic imagination. But if we are rigidly rationalist, we lose all those things that faith, hope and imagination can provide. Charles Wesley's verse is a foil to this. He speaks from experience, yet reaches beyond the compass of our senses to pierce the veil of heaven. And already I find myself speaking in the language of the mystics, florid and romantic, for this is where Wesley takes us, to touch the hem of the garment of God. And we've broken through the culture of our day that would deny the metaphysical. As we sing, we build our faith with greater confidence, expressing that trust which might lie dormant if unsung.

Wesley could take this path because his world view was determined by Scripture. That is not to say that he slavishly reproduced proof texts. Although a single hymn might contain upward of 40 Bible allusions, such was his skill that these would be woven one into another, so that the resulting text would have a clarity and unity rarely matched by lesser writers. All the time the priority of Scripture is underlined and the interpretation of Scripture is demonstrated.

Charles Wesley visited people in prison, cried out at the loss of his son to smallpox, yet initiated the Holy Club at Oxford to enable an ordered and methodical pursuit of prayer and faithful living. He preached wherever the crowds would listen, and wrote and wrote and wrote so that the Methodists might have a means to carry doctrine and Scripture with them wherever they went. This man was a true priest and prophet in touch with God and with people, always pointing people back to God.

In spite of all of this, it is true that much of Charles Wesley's language is of another age and his expression and understanding of faith came out of the culture of his day. But that is true of any writer of any age. Poetry has an advantage over prose. Good poetry can be a spring-board for the imagination. A word or a phrase catches our mind and we wander away from the printed page to thoughts of our own. When the poetry is religious this can lead us into prayer or devotion, meditation and mystical experience. For this reason alone it would be worth keeping Wesley's verse alive. Since the beginning of Methodism, Methodist Christians have used hymnody for devotional reading. John Keble, the Anglican Tractarian, produced a collection of verses, *The Christian Year*, to the same end. Frederick Faber, who became a Roman Catholic, understood that hymns could be used in this way. Until 1983, Methodists continued to use their hymns and their hymn books in this way, some singing a hymn a day through the book, or using it for reading or prayer. The Congregationalist, Bernard Lord Manning, commented on the practice in his lectures published as *The Hymns of Wesley and Watts*. The coming of newer hymn books laid out in a more liturgical way, together with a change in the language of many hymns, has made this practice less prevalent in recent years, but it is a habit worth exploring or revisiting and, with a bit of research, it is possible to find hymns both old and new that will stimulate our devotion and lead us into fresh avenues of prayer. Let this collection be a starting point.

I hope this book will be a source of blessing to those who share it and that, in an age in which these hymns are used less frequently, it will act as a reminder of the depth of faith and the poetic skill of Charles Wesley.

How to use this book

Most people confronted with a book like this will first look to see if their favourite hymn is there! I hope yours is. You can dip and choose as you see fit.

In Methodism using hymns as a form of devotion has a long tradition going back, we can imagine, to the practice of its founding fathers. Frederick Faber and John Keble, both nineteenth-century Anglicans (Faber later became a Roman Catholic) adopted this practice and wrote collections of hymns, some of which could only be easily used devotionally, as they were too long or personal to be sung by a congregation. So if you read hymns for your devotions you are following in a fine and diverse tradition of spirituality.

If you want to use the book in a more structured way it is worth reading a hymn a week. The devotional notes with each hymn can act as a starting point for you. These can, I hope, inspire your prayers or enable your meditation. You may like to look at a verse each day through the week – when there are sufficient verses – or go to your own hymn book and, having used this book to set your theme, look for other hymns that echo it.

The 52 hymns will take you through the year one week at a time. But where to start? After the first hymn in the book we progress through Advent. The rest of the year follows. Because parts of the Christian calendar change from year to year, and Easter can be early or late, the book is broken into sections which enable you to move through the seasons more easily. You might note any hymns that get missed and return to them in what some denominations call Ordinary Time, when there are no specific or particular festivals to mark.

The texts of the hymns

Hymn texts have been taken, sometimes with amendment, from *HymnQuest 2006*. Charles Wesley wrote many thousands of lines of verse and some of his hymn texts comprise many verses. On occasion long hymns have been broken into shorter units and, from time to time, it seems that a verse from one hymn has migrated into another. Added to this is the problem, which many hymn writers face, of self-quotation. In deciding on which version of a text to use I have chosen, for the most part, to use versions which are in current use at the time of writing. In doing this I have sometimes edited texts to make them more acceptable to modern congregations.

Nevertheless, the biggest problem facing an editor in producing a collection of hymns from this period is the use of non-inclusive language. While I am sensitive to this, and it is most prominent in terms of gender, I have chosen to amend the hymns minimally. They stand or fall as poetry of their age with all the pitfalls this entails. It is the responsibility of those using the hymns to use them sensitively, and for those writing hymns today to be aware that inclusivity is a natural extension of Wesley's 'gospel for all' Arminian theology.

In the beginning

1.   Away with our fears!

It is 18 December 1707 and in the rectory in the village of Epworth in Lincolnshire, Susanna Wesley is giving birth to a genius. His older brother John had come into the world some four years before. The birth we celebrate and remember is that of Charles Wesley, the greatest, perhaps the most prolific, hymn writer the world has ever known. His family were steeped in the Christian faith; his father was Rector. Through his education at Westminster School and Christ Church, Oxford, he was to develop a skill which few, if any, have matched.

There had been hymn writers before, Isaac Watts for one, but Charles lifted his art to a higher plain, as we shall see as we read through his words, and perhaps sing some! As I write hymns in the twenty-first century, his craft still challenges me to grapple with theology and to make faith relevant. The task of the hymn writer since the time of Charles Wesley has constantly been to provide a reminder of what we believe that can be carried in our heads and given expression in our singing.

Many years ago I stayed with the Sisters of Jesus' Way who ran a retreat house. If a guest had a birthday during their stay we sang this hymn:

1. Away with our fears!
   The glad morning appears
   When an heir of salvation was born!
   From Jehovah I came,
   For his glory I am,
   And to him I with singing return.

2. I sing of thy grace,
   From my earliest days
   Ever near to allure and defend;

Hitherto thou hast been
My preserver from sin,
And I trust thou wilt save to the end.

3. O the infinite cares,
And temptations, and snares
Thy hand has conducted me through!
O the blessings bestowed
By a bountiful God,
And the mercies eternally new!

4. What a mercy is this,
What a heaven of bliss,
How unspeakably happy am I,
Gathered into the fold,
With thy people enrolled,
With thy people to live and to die.

5. All honour and praise
To the Father of grace,
To the Spirit, and Son, I return;
The business pursue
He has made me to do,
And rejoice that I ever was born.

6. In a rapture of joy
My life I employ
The God of my life to proclaim;
'Tis worth living for, this,
To administer bliss,
And salvation in Jesus's name.

7. My remnant of days
I spend in his praise,
Who died the whole world to redeem:
Be they many or few,
My days are his due,
And they all are devoted to him.

Advent

2.   Lo, he comes with clouds descending

Let us sing our way through the year.

Part of the understanding that we have of religious story is the way it follows the calendar. This is not just a random whim, but a means of reminding us of God's action in human history and the birth of Jesus at a real point in time. Don't get me wrong. I know we can't be sure of exact dates, but we shouldn't lose track of the reality of events that we commemorate. If we do we risk watering down our understanding of God's relationship with us. Selling Christmas cards in August doesn't help our understanding!

So we enter Advent, and the darkness of the season, in the northern hemisphere, is accentuated. Candles are extinguished and we begin to prepare for the coming of the Light of the World. This season is filled with Old Testament images of the majesty and greatness, the wonder and magnificence of God. This is a time to focus on God's judgement and yet the hope of humanity in the face of that judgement.

The expected Messiah is pictured as coming on the clouds of heaven to take God's people home. Thousands of saints, holy people who have died through the ages, are imagined as being with him. The whole earth responds, every island, continent and nation. Meanwhile those who crucified Jesus are brought to judgement.

This is the final moment, the time when, it is envisaged, we come face to face with who we really are and all we have done, for good or ill. It is a time when all are called to adore God and to welcome Jesus back again into their midst, for 'Lo, he comes with clouds descending'.

1. Lo, he comes with clouds descending,
   Once for favoured sinners slain;
   Thousand thousand saints attending
   Swell the triumph of his train:
   Alleluia!
   God appears on earth to reign.

2. Every eye shall now behold him
   Robed in dreadful majesty;
   Those who set at naught and sold him,
   Pierced and nailed him to the tree,
   Deeply wailing,
   Shall the true Messiah see.

3 Those dear tokens of his passion
   Still his dazzling body bears;
   Cause of endless exultation
   To his ransomed worshippers:
   With what rapture
   Gaze we on those glorious scars.

4. Now redemption, long expected,
   See in solemn pomp appear:
   All his saints, by men rejected,
   Now shall meet him in the air:
   Alleluia!
   See the day of God appear.

5. Every island, sea, and mountain,
   Heaven and earth, shall flee away;
   All who hate him must, defeated,
   Hear his voice proclaim the day.
   Come to judgement!
   Come to judgement! come away.

6. Yea, amen, let all adore thee,
   High on thine eternal throne;
   Saviour, take the power and glory,
   Claim the kingdom for thine own:
   Come, Lord Jesus!
   Everlasting God, come down!

3.   Come, Holy Ghost, our hearts inspire

For me the second Sunday of Advent is still Bible Sunday. That got me thinking.

Browsing through my local bookshop I found numerous volumes about religion. Some of the books were conventional enough, titles I'd been brought up on, various translations of the Bible, some prayer books, an anthology of hymns. Then there was a Qu'ran, an introduction to Buddhism, a splendidly produced book by the Dalai Lama and, alongside these, books on tarot card reading and crystal healing. There were many more, yet these samples show well enough what a thirst people have for spiritual things. But I can hear some people muttering 'dangerous', or 'They're not Christian.' Still others bemoan the lack of interest in the Bible, or that few people come to church.

Ah, well. Part of the problem is that religious books have had a bad press, and the way religious people use their Scriptures is a large part of the problem. Books which were written in a particular context millennia ago need to be understood and interpreted in the light of that time and place. When one part of a collection of books seems to be at odds with another part, as is so often the case with the Bible, we need to admit the contradiction and to account for it. To take the Bible as indisputable, literal truth does a disservice to the undoubted truths it does contain.

So what do we need to do? John and Charles Wesley, using the scholarship and faith of their day, offered some answers. John Wesley produced *Explanatory Notes on the New Testament* in an attempt to explain it. He suggested that if a part of Scripture seemed difficult to understand another part might make it clearer. Charles came from another direction. He knew that people had written the Bible, prophets for instance, but he believed that they had been inspired by God. If that were so, that same God could unlock these truths for us and for this Charles prayed.

1. Come, Holy Ghost, our hearts inspire,
   Let us thine influence prove;
   Source of the old prophetic fire,
   Fountain of life and love.

2. Come, Holy Ghost (for moved by thee
   The prophets wrote and spoke),
   Unlock the truth, thyself the key,
   Unseal the sacred book.

3. Expand thy wings, celestial dove,
   Brood o'er our nature's night;
   On our disordered spirits move,
   And let there now be light.

4. God through himself we then shall know,
   If thou within us shine;
   And sound, with all thy saints below,
   The depths of love divine.

4. Come, thou long-expected Jesus

I remember as a child the excitement of the circus or the fair coming to town. A couple of weeks before there would be signs round the town. By today's standards they were primitive, small sheets of paper printed in, at most, two colours, a few pictures and some words, always a date. To childlike eyes they breathed excitement and expectation. Then some days before the due date lots of lorries, tractors, caravans, people would start to arrive. Stalls or a tent were erected on the green. 'Don't go there, it's dangerous,' warned my mother. She was not worried, in those days, that the people were untrustworthy, rather that men with heavy machinery, ropes and pulleys all concentrating on their business might not notice a little lad and he might get hurt. Then the big day came and we'd go and queue to see the high-wire artists and to get a glimpse of the clowns. Or if it was a fair we looked at the colourful roundabouts, favoured by my mum but which made me sick, the boxing for dad and the bumper cars for me. All the waiting was always worthwhile and it was sad when these special visitors packed up and moved on for another year.

In Jesus' day the coming of a preacher could stir up as much excitement, even more so if he was a bit out of the ordinary. The word had been going around that a wild man living in the desert was coming down to the River Jordan. What he had to say was worth hearing. All the people from the surrounding towns went out to him. For some it was just what they had been waiting for. He understood the plight of those who were downtrodden. To them his words were comfortable, but those in power who risked going along with the crowd heard a different message. The religious leaders and politicians (there was little to choose between them), were a 'brood of vipers', hypocrites. There were mixed feelings amongst that gathering.

John was baptizing people. Anyone who wanted to make a fresh start was invited to come down into the river, to duck down as though they were drowning, to rise up again to a symbolic new life. In the middle of the crowd was Jesus, quietly insignificant, though John recognized him. 'I baptize you with water ... but one who is more powerful than I is coming after me; I am not worthy to carry his sandals. He will baptize you with the Holy Spirit and fire' (Matthew 3.11–12).

And still we sing, 'Come, thou long-expected Jesus'. And when he comes, this healer, this comforter, this exciter of souls, he will never pack up and go away again, will never turn his face from you.

1. Come, thou long-expected Jesus,
   Born to set thy people free,
   From our fears and sins release us,
   Let us find our rest in thee.

2. Israel's strength and consolation,
   Hope of all the earth thou art;
   Dear desire of every nation,
   Joy of every longing heart.

3. Born thy people to deliver,
   Born a child and yet a king,
   Born to reign in us for ever,
   Now thy gracious kingdom bring.

4. By thine own eternal Spirit
   Rule in all our hearts alone;
   By thine all-sufficient merit
   Raise us to thy glorious throne.

5. Behold the servant of the Lord!

Travelling is risky. If you go by train or fly, take a taxi or go by bus you put yourself in the hands of the driver or pilot. You trust in their training and skill. You assume that they are going to be properly prepared, that they will be well-rested, that they haven't been drinking. Settling down, you enjoy the journey and, if you're a seasoned traveller, you don't think twice. Of course, not everyone is like that. Some people have a phobia about flying; for others past experience of an accident may make travelling on a bus feel impossible. The first time you fly there is usually a sense of at least slight trepidation. Putting yourself in someone else's hands is a risky business.

How much more risky it is for a baby being born? The infant is at the whim of those who carry her, those who feed him, those who care and comfort, the ones who teach, who love or scold. And the child has no choice, just arrives! What a responsibility for parents!

So the story goes, God spoke to a young woman and said, 'I am going to be born and you are going to be my mother.' Bit stark that, isn't it? But, in effect, that is what happened when Mary heard that she was going to give birth to Jesus, if we take the Christian story at face value. We usually think of Jesus being betrayed by Judas. The literal meaning of the Greek word used here means 'handed over'. In reality Jesus was handed over to humanity at his birth. God took the risk of trusting a young girl with his human nurture and care. Mary accepted that role as parent, a role that would have it's full share of human joy and sorrow.

When Charles Wesley wrote the words, 'Mould as thou wilt thy passive clay' I do not believe he thought of himself as having no self-determination or that he was giving up his own free will. Neither did he expect to be abused. He assumed that this parent God would take ultimate, particular care of him and, in the light of God's steadfast loving kindness, he was willing to say, 'I am no longer my own but yours, put me to what you will.' Words of trust, words of dedication. Can we echo them?

1. Behold the servant of the Lord!
   I wait thy guiding eye to feel,
   To hear and keep thy every word,
   To prove and do thy perfect will,
   Joyful from my own works to cease,
   Glad to fulfil all righteousness.

2. Me if thy grace vouchsafe to use,
   Meanest of all thy creatures, me,
   The deed, the time, the manner choose;
   Let all my fruit be found of thee;
   Let all my works in thee be wrought,
   By thee to full perfection brought.

3. My every weak though good design
   O'errule or change, as seems thee meet;
   Jesus, let all my work be thine!
   Thy work, O Lord, is all complete,
   And pleasing in thy Father's sight;
   Thou only hast done all things right.

4. Here then to thee thine own I leave;
   Mould as thou wilt thy passive clay;
   But let me all thy stamp receive,
   But let me all thy words obey,
   Serve with a single heart and eye,
   And to thy glory live and die.

Christmas

6.   Hark, the herald-angels sing

How can we sum up this most wonderful belief, that God cares for each one of us completely, totally, forever? How can we communicate our wonder that God in Jesus was willing to die rather than to deny that love to any human being, even those who had nailed him to a cross? How can we give expression to the sense of peace and hope and love with which we want to respond at the high points in our faith when we feel utterly loved by God and at one with the world and our neighbours?

Charles Wesley wrote:

> Hark, how all the welkin rings,
> 'Glory to the King of kings;
> peace on earth, and mercy mild,
> God and sinners reconciled!'

The words sound strange but they sum up that overwhelming sense of wonder, love and praise which we've been stumbling towards. The word 'welkin' meant 'the heavens' and Wesley imagines that all the songs of earth are not enough to give expression to the amazement that he feels. This is the peak of all the faith he has ever felt. His 'heart is free'; he knows firsthand that God's love is a 'love divine, all loves excelling'; he feels that a flame has been kindled, a flame of 'sacred love on the mean altar of [his] heart'. A 'thousand tongues' will not sing loudly enough, tunefully enough to sound his 'great redeemer's praise'. For Wesley nothing short of the choirs of heaven are enough, and the whole of heaven, he imagines, rings to the chorus as Jesus is born. Surely nothing less is sufficient?

I envy Wesley's simplicity and clarity of expression. So, as we sing with the angels, remember the welkin and know that all of heaven joins our praise to welcome in the 'new-born king'.

1. Hark, the herald-angels sing
   Glory to the new-born King,
   Peace on earth, and mercy mild,
   God and sinners reconciled.
   Joyful, all ye nations, rise,
   Join the triumph of the skies;
   With the angelic host proclaim,
   'Christ is born in Bethlehem.'
   Hark, the herald-angels sing
   Glory to the new-born King.

2. Christ, by highest heaven adored,
   Christ, the everlasting Lord,
   Late in time behold him come,
   Offspring of a Virgin's womb.
   Veiled in flesh the Godhead see:
   Hail, the incarnate Deity,
   Pleased as man with man to dwell,
   Jesus, our Emmanuel.
   Hark, the herald-angels sing
   Glory to the new-born King.

3. Hail, the heaven-born Prince of Peace:
   Hail, the Sun of Righteousness.
   Light and life to all he brings,
   Risen with healing in his wings.
   Mild he lays his glory by,
   Born that man no more may die,
   Born to raise the sons of earth,
   Born to give them second birth.
   Hark, the herald-angels sing
   Glory to the new-born King.

7.   Sing to the great Jehovah's praise

And now the nights are dark. We've just passed the shortest day. I wonder how you feel at this time. Some people are genuinely depressed. Others look forward with hope to a new year that will be better than the last. Charles begins by thanking God for adding another year to his life, for bringing him through another year. Whatever happened last year for you or me, this is still relevant if we value life. The lengthening of our days, food, shelter, life itself can be a sign of God's providence. That is how Charles came to see it. A simple faith, but not one to be easily dismissed; a faith that has inspired and carried Christians the world over.

Life is not always easy. Personal tragedy affects us. We are aware of tidal waves and earthquakes and perhaps we have experienced them first-hand. Conflict and aggression affect our world, our streets, perhaps even our own families. At the turning of the year we look back on what might have been. We reflect on the bad things that have happened, as well as the good. Our very survival is a reason for Charles to believe in God's mercy and continuing care. 'Count your blessings' someone else was to write at a later date. That's what it's all about. The year may have had more than its fair share of grief and illness but you are still here. God has kept you, has kept me, with some purpose for this coming year. That's a reason to praise God: not only are we here but we are here with a purpose.

For Charles Wesley, that purpose was recognized indisputably from the earliest years. In his early sermons he underlines the need for the Christian to persevere in discipleship, to strive for heaven, to work for God. So, as the old year ends and the new one begins, Charles takes the opportunity to rededicate himself to God and God's purposes in the most wholehearted way possible. And so should we!

1. Sing to the great Jehovah's praise;
   All praise to him belongs;
   Who kindly lengthens out our days
   Demands our choicest songs.

2. His providence has brought us through
   Another various year;
   We all with vows and anthems new
   Before our God appear.

3. Father, thy mercies past we own,
   Thy still continued care;
   To thee presenting, through thy Son,
   Whate'er we have or are.

4. Our lips and lives shall gladly show
   The wonders of thy love,
   While on in Jesus' steps we go
   To see thy face above.

5. Our residue of days or hours
   Thine, wholly thine, shall be,
   And all our consecrated powers
   A sacrifice to thee.

New Year and Epiphany

8.   Come, let us anew

The end of one year, the beginning of another. To look back was to thank God for preservation and providence. But Charles Wesley knew that the Christian was never to stand still. Jesus once said, 'My *food* is to do the will of him who sent me and to complete his work' (John 4.34). You eat and drink or you die. So it is with the active life of the Christian. Its essence is activity. Once having put your hand to the plough the way is forward. The spread of Methodism worldwide is witness to the Wesleys' personal commitment to this task.

We are invited and challenged to recognize the gifts and talents God has given us. The life of the poet, however, can sometimes be seen as remote and introspective. It can be very selfish, to cut yourself off and 'do your work'. It can be an arrogant pastime. The other side of the coin is what Charles certainly recognized, that if you have a gift it should be used to the full to the service of humanity. If he had not taken that to heart the Christian Church would have been so much the poorer, both in what it sang and in the lasting influence that he and his brother John shed down the centuries.

So there is a responsibility placed on us all to know and use our gifts in the working out of God's will. We have to grasp the moment, take up the labour of love in our own situation. No time can or must be wasted until our task is done, and, if we're still alive, arguably our role here is not yet finished.

Only at the end can we expect to hear the words, 'Well done, good and faithful servant'. Only then can we lay down our tools, put aside our work, cease our prayer, 'Cast our crowns before thee, lost in wonder love and praise'. Until then we have a journey ahead of us.

1. Come, let us anew
   Our journey pursue,
   Roll round with the year,
   And never stand still till the Master appear.

2. His adorable will
   Let us gladly fulfil,
   And our talents improve,
   By the patience of hope and the labour of love.

3. Our life is a dream,
   Our time as a stream
   Glides swiftly away,
   And the fugitive moment refuses to stay.

4. The arrow is flown,
   The moment is gone;
   The millennial year
   Rushes on to our view, and eternity's here.

5. O that each in the day,
   Of his coming may say:
   'I have fought my way through,
   I have finished the work thou didst give me to do!'

6. O that each from his Lord
   May receive the glad word:
   'Well and faithfully done;
   Enter into my joy, and sit down on my throne!'

9. Let earth and heaven combine

So the baubles and decorations have been put away. If you had a tree I wonder what you've done with it? Into the new year we go. For Christians this is a time of trying to make sense of the baby born in a stable. A celebration of the coming of wise men, of kings, to a humble dwelling. What do we make of it all?

My recollection over the years is that this season of Epiphany is lost in new year sales, amid getting back to work. Then, at a religious level it's about the trumpeting of the media who have feasted on a bishop who has had the courage to voice his doubts about the Virgin Birth.

Amid all this I have the echo at the back of my mind of a phrase from a hymn, 'Our God contracted to a span, incomprehensibly made man'. As a writer am I allowed to envy Wesley's way with words, the economy of his language? I can certainly learn from him! This text is not as well known as some but, as ever, he gets to the nub of the matter and his conclusion is as important today as it ever was: that 'God came down at Christmas'.

Even those of us who are religious can lose sight of that at one level or another. We can get caught up in the theological conundrums and explanations of the Virgin Birth. We can sentimentalize about the child who is 'away in a manger'. In all of these we miss the point that Charles Wesley underlines again and again: the angels heralded the coming of God. The baby in the manger was God.

Why does it matter? Because when you or I pray we are not firing words at clouds or harassing a detached deity, we are talking to 'Our God, contracted to a span, incomprehensibly made man'. We are pleading with a God who understands human weakness through personal experience. And at times of utter desolation we are heard by a forsaken God who hung on a cross outside the city and outside the society that had rejected him.

1. Let earth and heaven combine,
   Angels and men agree,
   To praise in songs divine
   The incarnate deity,
   Our God contracted to a span,
   Incomprehensibly made man.

2. He laid his glory by,
   He wrapped him in our clay,
   Unmarked by human eye,
   The latent Godhead lay;
   Infant of days he here became,
   And bore the mild Immanuel's name.

3. See in that infant's face
   The depth of Deity,
   And labour while ye gaze
   To sound the mystery:
   In vain; ye angels, gaze no more,
   But fall, and silently adore.

4. Unsearchable the love
   That has the Saviour brought;
   The grace is far above
   Or men or angels' thought:
   Suffice for us that God, we know,
   Our God, is manifest below.

5. He deigns in flesh to appear,
   Widest extremes to join;
   To bring our vileness near,
   To make us all divine:
   And we the life of God shall know,
   For God is manifest below.

6. Made perfect first in love,
   And sanctified by grace,
   We shall from earth remove,
   And see his glorious face:
   His love shall then be fully showed,
   And man shall all be lost in God.

Good news for all

10. O thou, whom once they flocked to hear

There is a fashionable form of spirituality attributed to St Ignatius Loyola which, at its simplest level, asks us to imagine ourselves as characters in the stories of Jesus. Try it sometime if you haven't done already. What was it like to be in the crowd by the lakeside? How did it feel to be like Philip, keeper of the purse, when Jesus suggests they might feed 5,000 hungry people? What was it like for strong, confident Peter, just when he'd recognized Jesus as Messiah on the Mount of Transfiguration, to be called 'Satan'? It makes you think, and the places and the people come alive, and we can feel ourselves among the crowds flocking to hear Jesus, seeing him and hearing his words. In Korea or the Americas, in Australia or the Caribbean your picture may be different, your culture will affect your imagining, but God reaches each of us nevertheless.

Imagination can bring us closer to the reality of those stories and one consequence is the realization that what happened then might happen again now. I'm not asking you to throw away a view of the world that is 21 centuries detached from the time in which Jesus lived, but I am suggesting that it is very easy for us just to read these stories as history. Once we've got ourselves back into them, so to speak, we understand that what people faced then in their day-to-day lives was not much different from what we face now. Babies were born and people died. Sometimes they were ill. Those who were different because of some disability or infirmity were ostracized; the world belonged to the strong and the powerful. But as we get inside the stories we find Jesus welcoming mothers with babies, offering hope and healing to those who were sick. Those who were regarded as worthless because of their appearance or disability, Jesus included. Those who were feared because they were foreign, he used as an example of human and divine love. Those who had done wrong and broken the rules of society, he forgave.

Gradually, or sometimes in a blinding flash, we realize that if that was how Jesus was then, that is how God is now. It is a comforting realization when we are in desperate need ourselves. As Charles Wesley knew and we should understand, this is a message for every place and time. It is for now. And as for Jesus, his life is a stunning challenge to us all as we seek to live in harmony with those around us. What an example!

1. O thou, whom once they flocked to hear,
   Thy words to hear, thy power to feel;
   Suffer the sinners to draw near,
   And graciously receive us still.

2. They that be whole, thyself hast said,
   No need of a physician have;
   But I am sick, and want thine aid,
   And ask thine utmost power to save.

3. Thy power, and truth, and love divine,
   The same from age to age endure;
   A word, a gracious word of thine,
   The most inveterate plague can cure.

4. Helpless howe'er my spirit lies,
   And long hath languished at the pool,
   A word of thine shall make me rise,
   Shall speak me in a moment whole.

5. Make this my Lord's accepted hour;
   Come, O my soul's physician thou!
   Display thy justifying power,
   And show me thy salvation now.

11. Come, divine Interpreter

Imagination is not the only way towards understanding the Bible. I don't know which version of the Bible you use or even in which language it is printed. The days are long gone when we could assume that everyone was familiar with just one version. In my childhood I remember my mother extolling the worth of a particular minister. His main virtue was that he used J.B. Phillips' translation of the New Testament. Mum could understand that and she revelled in it, buying her own copy – sadly lost in house moves years ago – though I still have that translation on my own shelves. Each generation now seems to be offered more and more options and in addition to children's Bibles there are those for young people, and for men or women. What on earth do we make of all this?

Part of the problem is that the Bible wasn't written in our language. Translations cannot always pick up subtle nuances of meaning. One person's perspective is not the same as another's. Matthew, Mark, Luke and John saw Jesus through different eyes. So how can we make sense of Scripture? One way forward is simply to assume that it is God's word, inspired by God without error. But there are those places where one passage contradicts another. John Wesley suggested that if a particular passage was difficult it could sometimes be explained by reference to another. For instance we are told to 'Love the Lord your God with all your heart, and with all your soul, and with all your mind' (Matthew 22.37); but also that 'Those who say "I love God", and hate their brothers or sisters, are liars' (1 John 4.20). One passage helps us make sense of the other. Whether or not we love our brother, or indeed our sister, is a pretty good test of our love of God.

There are still occasions though when, however hard we try, we can't make sense of the Bible. Charles Wesley wrote a hymn which we can use as a prayer in this sort of situation and it's useful whenever we study the Bible. His argument went like this: if God inspired the writers of the Bible, then everyone who tries to make sense of the Bible should go back to that same God for help in understanding. Then, in the light of God making the words plain to us, we will be blessed. That makes sense. And the offer seems good to me.

1. Come, divine Interpreter,
   Bring us eyes thy book to read,
   Ears the mystic words to hear,
   Words which did from thee proceed,
   Words that endless bliss impart,
   Kept in an obedient heart.

2. All who read, or hear, are blessed,
   If thy plain commands we do;
   Of thy kingdom here possessed,
   Thee we shall in glory view –
   When thou com'st on earth to abide,
   Reign triumphant at thy side.

Ash Wednesday

12. What shall I do my God to love

I wonder who your friends are and what they're like? If I think of the people that I get on with, with whom I want to share time, they are the ones who share my interests first and foremost. I love conversation and I have to start somewhere. I'm utterly at a loss with small talk. Put me in a party and I want to merge with the wallpaper! I remember going to a wedding once, where my cousin was the mother of the bride. Now she has a gift, or her daughter does. We found ourselves sitting by people who had many of the same interests and experiences. They were about our age, remembered the same events, and knew some of the same people. That made it easier for me. I don't know how I'd find them in the long run, but that didn't matter. The meal was good. The conversation flowed. The experience was pleasant.

To deepen a relationship beliefs and values have to come into play. That's why religion and politics are so often taboo – subjects that can raise passions and bring about disagreements. Even people we think are like ourselves can upset us and we can upset them – have you never been to a church council? And if we find others difficult, how do they find us? I sometimes wonder how God copes, having to deal with all of us! Yet that is the belief that drove Charles Wesley. This God whom he worshipped had the capacity to love the whole of humankind of every age and time. That was a matter of supreme wonder to him and it raised the question of how people should respond in return. It is a question which still ought to exercise us if this is what we believe. Ours is not a small-talking God but one who penetrates to the depths of our humanity. God knows us and understands us; sees us 'warts and all' as Cromwell might have said. Not only that but, God copes with those we do not love, those we despise, those we hate. I can understand God loving me. But you? When some people were trying to stone a woman who had committed adultery, Jesus recognized that attitude in them. It was as though he held up a mirror to them. 'Take a look at yourselves,' he seemed to say. And the crowd dispersed until only the woman was left. 'Does anyone condemn you,' asked Jesus. 'No one Lord,' she replied. 'Then neither do I condemn you,' responded Jesus.

I guess that woman knew that she had done wrong and she expected to be punished. But the love of God that we see in the person of Jesus is so broad that she was forgiven.

I think Charles Wesley must have felt a little like her. He felt that all the wrong in his life was piled up like a heap in front of him. He knew how wide God's love was and he rejoiced in being forgiven. For John Wesley that would have been enough. 'Forgiven, loved and free', – end of the story. But Charles was less certain. Not only was his sin like a great tower needing immense forgiveness but, as soon as he was forgiven, he sensed the need of forgiveness again. It was not that God had not cleared him and loved him but that he never lost the ability to do wrong, so day by day he needed God's grace afresh. And so do I. So it's Charles words we sing and not John's.

1. What shall I do my God to love,
   My loving God to praise?
   The length, and breadth, and height to prove,
   And depth of sovereign grace?

2. Thy sovereign grace to all extends,
   Immense and unconfined;
   From age to age it never ends;
   It reaches all mankind.

3. Throughout the world its breadth is known,
   Wide as infinity;
   So wide it never passed by one,
   Or it had passed by me.

4. My trespass *is* grown up to heaven;
   But, far above the skies,
   In Christ abundantly forgiven,
   I see thy mercies rise.

5. The depth of all-redeeming love
   What angel tongue can tell?
   O may I to the utmost prove
   The gift unspeakable!

6. Come quickly, gracious Lord, and take
   Possession of thine own;
   My longing heart vouchsafe to make
   Thine everlasting throne.

Lent

13. Pray, without ceasing pray

One of my favourite times of year is Lent. Don't get me wrong. I'm not one who gives up a lot in Lent. I was taken to task once by a Muslim for this, during Ramadan. He was fasting from sunrise to sunset. 'You do the same in Lent, don't you?' I had to admit that fasting was not one of my strong points. What he was getting at made me think. Traditionally Lent was the time for remembering Jesus' time in the wilderness, a time of temptation. The custom of eating pancakes on Shrove Tuesday began as the feast before the fast, eating up eggs, clearing the larder, a mirroring of our clearing of ourselves in preparation to share something of that wilderness experience with Jesus. The Church began to use the time for the preparation of people for baptism which would take place on Easter Sunday. For some (don't tell the children this), the identification with Jesus went as far as not having a bath through the whole of Lent!

Whatever the custom you keep, underlying this period of the Church year is the intention to spend more time in prayer, more time with God alone. So whatever your diet – make time for God. When we would be eating, we can be praying.

Charles Wesley recognized the importance of the command to pray. He linked it with Luke 18.1-8 where Jesus tells a story about a widow who pesters an unjust judge until she gets justice. Jesus' conclusion is that the Christian should be as persistent as the widow in prayer to God. Yet this prayer is never selfish, but always seeking peace, moving towards the coming of God's rule on earth. It is a prayer not just for ourselves but for the whole Church. This prayer does not come easily and is not without sacrifice and struggle.

In one sense all of our life should be a prayer. It follows, too, that prayer is not something private and ineffectual but active and political. I think both Wesley brothers would say 'Amen' to that! Perhaps we should stop more often to pray?

1. Pray, without ceasing pray,
   Your captain gives the word;
   His summons cheerfully obey,
   And call upon the Lord:
   To God your every want
   In instant prayer display;
   Pray always; pray, and never faint;
   Pray, without ceasing pray!

2. In fellowship, alone,
   To God with faith draw near,
   Approach his courts, besiege his throne
   With all the powers of prayer:
   Go to his temple, go,
   Nor from his altar move;
   Let every house his worship know
   And every heart his love.

3. Pour out your souls to God,
   And bow them with your knees,
   And spread your hearts and hands abroad,
   And pray for Zion's peace;
   Your guides and brethren bear
   For ever on your mind;
   Extend the arms of mighty prayer,
   In grasping all mankind.

4. From strength to strength go on,
   Wrestle, and fight, and pray,
   Tread all the powers of darkness down,
   And win the well-fought day;
   Still let the Spirit cry
   In all his soldiers: Come!
   Till Christ the Lord descend from high,
   And take the conquerors home.

14. From trials unexempted

It was Oscar Wilde who said, 'I can resist everything except temptation.' That's true for most of us. Usually the greater the prohibition the greater the temptation – 'Go on; see if you can get away with it!' You don't know the feeling? Honest? Well, many people do. And Jesus did. Matthew and Luke give us the details of Jesus' temptation in the wilderness but I have a feeling that wasn't Jesus' only time of temptation: 'Take this cup away from me, yet ...' that moment of uncertainty in the Garden of Gethsemane. And perhaps there were others times too. I find that helpful.

Charles Wesley was aware of the power of temptation but sensed that the best way to cope with it was by praying to God that we might not be tempted beyond what we can resist. He had a very strong sense of the necessity for the Christian to make every human effort possible to strive for perfection, but he also knew that it was human to fail. This is where faith steps in, not when we haven't bothered to make the effort, when we have been lackadaisical in striving to be good, but when, in spite of doing our best, we still fail. This is why, in spite of his failure, Jesus gave the keys of God's kingdom to Peter. This is why Jesus, after the resurrection, greeted the disciples with words of peace when they had run from his cross. If we succumb to temptation we do not fall beyond the scope of God's forgiveness and grace, or God's almighty love.

It is this that compels the Christian to greater acts of self-sacrificial love: the knowledge of the height and the depth, the length and the breadth of God's love. This love is great enough, deep enough, and wide enough to encompass every one of us. That makes me want to sing 'Alleluia!' even in the middle of Lent.

1. From trials unexempted
   Thy dearest children are;
   But let us not be tempted
   Above what we can bear;
   Exposed to no temptation
   That may our souls o'erpower,
   Be thou our strong salvation
   Through every fiery hour.

2. Ah! leave us not to venture
   Within the verge of sin;
   Or if the snare we enter,
   Thy timely help bring in;
   And if thy wisdom try us,
   Till pain and woe are past,
   Almighty Love, stand by us,
   And save from first to last.

3. Fain would we cease from sinning
   In thought, and word, and deed;
   From sin in its beginning
   We languish to be freed;
   From every base desire,
   Our fallen nature's shame,
   Jesus, we dare require
   Deliverance in thy name.

4. For every sinful action
   Thou hast atonement made,
   The perfect satisfaction
   Thy precious blood has paid:
   But take entire possession;
   To make an end of sin,
   To finish the transgression
   Most holy God, come in!

15. Ah! Lord, with trembling I confess

Anyone who has lived in a close relationship with another person for a long time will know that 'the course of true love never does run smooth'. You meet someone and you grow in knowledge and understanding. Sooner or later that leads you to a point of difference. How do you resolve that? I remember talking with a minister many years ago. 'I've never had a cross word with my wife,' he said. I wonder if he had ever talked to her! Not talking, hiding our differences is one way of coping. Others talk through what they believe, what they don't believe, and the things that impress and those that irritate. Sometimes they agree to differ; sometimes they seek to persuade the other to their point of view. Living peaceably with someone when you have spoken openly of your differences and recognized that they will not go away is a great gift.

I wonder if this very human experience was behind Charles Wesley's thought when he tried to work out in a hymn something of great significance. For some it seemed that if you had fallen in love with God that you could never fall out of love, no matter how you behaved. Such was God's faithfulness. But then you could do what you liked! Surely that was not right. Yet, if God's love was as great as Charles Wesley believed, God could forgive anything and anyone. There was a contradiction here.

Burying our heads in the sand does not lead to reconciliation or heal difficulties. Talking them through can. Sometimes we say sorry, sometimes we can't, but the issues are out in the open. Such openness is possible with the God that Charles had come to love. He knew that he should strive to be as good as he could. He knew that relationships between people can shatter. Equally we can break away from God. We never have total licence to do as we please in any relationship. Through prayerful conversation with God understanding grows. Nothing is hidden. Love becomes more firmly rooted. We move through times of apparent distance and tension to the heights of wonder. The youthful love that once we knew can be kindled again. Pray for that!

1. Ah! Lord, with trembling I confess,
   A gracious soul may fall from grace:
   The salt may lose its seasoning power,
   And never, never find it more.

2. Lest that my fearful case should be,
   Each moment knit my soul to thee;
   And lead me to the mount above,
   Through the low vale of humble love.

16. None is like Jeshurun's God

Have you ever had a nickname, a pet name? I've had a few in my life and I'm not about to tell you what they were now! Sometimes names like that can be hurtful. Sometimes they are descriptive: Tractarians issued tracts, Methodists were methodical in their worship, fellowship and prayer. The best names of this sort signify affection, the sort of names that lovers use for each other in private when no one else is listening. They convey a sense of intimacy, of possession sometimes, or being possessed, in the best possible way. This is the name that only she uses of you, only you use of him. No, you needn't confess what it is!

In the King James Version of the Old Testament Israel is sometimes, though very rarely, called Jeshurun: 'There is none like unto the God of *Jeshurun*, who rideth upon the heaven in thy help, and in his excellency on the sky' (Deuteronomy 33.26).

This was a very special name, God's pet name for the chosen people, if you like. These people were immensely precious to God, so precious that Charles Wesley, quoting Deuteronomy, sees God coming from heaven to earth in their aid. He believes that all the people in the world are the heirs to salvation promised to Israel. So Jeshurun's God becomes our God.

Have you ever felt the need to know that someone cares for you and will protect you? Have you ever needed to be reassured of the strength of God's love and protection? If so, these words can be words of immense comfort. At another level, if you've ever sung the children's song 'My God is so big', waving your hands in the air, doing all the actions, but now age and decorum has stiffened you, then this could be the hymn for you!

1. None is like Jeshurun's God,
   So great, so strong, so high;
   Lo! He spreads his wings abroad,
   He rides upon the sky:
   Israel is his first-born son;
   God, the almighty God, is thine;
   See him to thy help come down,
   The excellence divine.

2. Thee the great Jehovah deigns
   To succour and defend;
   Thee the eternal God sustains,
   Thy Maker and thy Friend:
   Israel, what hast thou to dread?
   Safe from all impending harms,
   Round thee and beneath are spread
   The everlasting arms.

3. God is thine; disdain to fear
   The enemy within:
   God shall in thy flesh appear,
   And make an end of sin;
   God the man of sin shall slay,
   Fill thee with triumphant joy;
   God shall thrust him out, and say:
   Destroy them all, destroy!

4. All the struggle then is o'er,
   And wars and fightings cease;
   Israel then shall sin no more,
   But dwell in perfect peace:
   All his enemies are gone;
   Sin shall have in him no part;
   Israel now shall dwell alone,
   With Jesus in his heart.

5. Blest, O Israel, art thou!
   What people is like thee?
   Saved from sin by Jesus, now
   Thou art and still shalt be;
   Jesus is thy sevenfold shield,
   Jesus is thy flaming sword;
   Earth, and hell, and sin shall yield
   To God's almighty Word.

17. Come on, my partners in distress

Sometimes life is boring. We just feel as though we are going on and on with no purpose. Day follows day and it can all seem a bit bleak. Then again, at a time of bereavement, it can feel as though the world keeps on revolving and no one has noticed the grief we feel. People can be very insensitive at times. Like W.H Auden, we want to cry for the clocks to be stopped, for someone to notice what has happened to us. It can make you want to scream!

When his son was dying of smallpox, Wesley wrote a poem which begins with a reference to Isaac who had been taken up the mountain by his father and was going to be killed as an offering. At the moment of sacrifice a ram is seen caught in the bushes and Abraham, as it were, receives back his son. Charles identifies with this story. With great emotion he cries out, 'For pity's sake the victim spare/And give me back my son'. The words are individual and extremely personal, yet for the person who sees his/her child dying, 'their best piece of poetry', the questions are eternal and the lament universal. Like any parent Charles seeks to understand the incomprehensible, to give reason to the irrational. It is so easy to think that people from history were different from us but we are all human and some emotions are universal. So when Charles spoke of grief he knew what he was talking about.

When we suffer it is good to be reminded that God is present with us in the suffering. This is not a false claim but one backed up by the experience of generations. We are not alone. When we go beyond that point, not because we have got over the grief, but because we cannot get over it, the idea that God will ultimately greet us, enfold us in love and welcome us home, as it were, can be a comfort. Not 'pie in the sky when you die' but an assurance that there is nothing that can separate us from the love of God. In the age in which we live such claims are easy to sweep away. Perhaps they only make sense when there is nothing else left to hope for, when we are grasping at straws and suddenly become aware of the reality that God is, in effect, reaching out for us – sublime hope!

1. Come on, my partners in distress,
   My comrades through the wilderness,
   Who still your bodies feel;
   Awhile forget your griefs and fears,
   And look beyond this vale of tears
   To that celestial hill.

2. Beyond the bounds of time and space,
   Look forward to that heavenly place,
   The saints' secure abode:
   On faith's strong eagle-pinions rise,
   And force your passage to the skies,
   And scale the mount of God.

3. Who suffer with our Master here,
   We shall before his face appear,
   And by his side sit down;
   To patient faith the prize is sure,
   And all that to the end endure
   The cross, shall wear the crown.

4. Thrice blessèd, bliss-inspiring hope!
   It lifts the fainting spirits up,
   It brings to life the dead;
   Our conflicts here shall soon be past,
   And you and I ascend at last,
   Triumphant with our Head.

5. That great mysterious Deity
   We soon with open face shall see;
   The beatific sight
   Shall fill heaven's sounding courts with praise,
   And wide diffuse the golden blaze
   Of everlasting light.

6. The Father shining on his throne,
   The glorious co-eternal Son,
   The spirit, one and seven,
   Conspire our rapture to complete:
   And lo! we fall before his feet,
   And silence heightens heaven.

7. In hope of that ecstatic pause,
   Jesus, we now sustain the cross,
   And at thy footstool fall;
   Till thou our hidden life reveal,
   Till thou our ravished spirits fill,
   And God is all in all.

Holy Week and Easter

18. Jesus, we thus obey

Memories! Now there's a cue for a song! Seriously, though, memories are so precious. If we realized that everything we did today was going to prepare memories for tomorrow, perhaps we'd be a little bit more careful.

What do you remember best? They say that you forget pain; physical pain maybe. But some of my sharpest memories are of events that hurt the most, things I've said to others and then seen their response. Then again there have been things that others have said to me, of which I've only later recognized the truth. We make memories for each other. A baby looking up from its mother's arms, the first faltering steps of a toddler, the lingering kiss of lovers; memories are made of so many different things and they touch our emotions, prompt our tears and charge our lives with laughter.

And on the night of the Last Supper Jesus said to them, 'Do this in remembrance of me.' Those words have echoed down the ages from generation to generation. The story has been told and retold. In every century Christians have heard it, re-enacted it and found their place in it. The memory has been carried by the Church.

What about us today? Remember the characters who were present. Peter was not only a rock but a hot-headed rebel, who did not always get it right. The story of the feeding of the 5,000 has Philip acting like the worst kind of treasurer: 'How can we afford to feed all these!' Remember how Thomas doubted and Judas betrayed Jesus. All these people, with their oh-so-human foibles, gathered round that table. They all shared. None was left out – a parable for our times, perhaps. Jesus shared most closely with the one who would betray him.

So we gather, welcoming all to an open table, conscious of our unworthiness yet not that of any other. Here we sit, we kneel or we stand because we too wish to obey 'Thy last and kindest word'.

1. Jesus, we thus obey
   Thy last and kindest word;
   Here, in thine own appointed way,
   We come to meet thee, Lord.

2. Our hearts we open wide
   To make the Saviour room;
   And lo! The Lamb, the crucified,
   The sinner's friend, is come!

3. His presence makes the feast;
   And now our spirits feel
   The glory not to be expressed,
   The joy unspeakable.

4. With pure celestial bliss
   He doth our spirits cheer;
   His house of banqueting is this,
   And he hath brought us here.

5. Now let our souls be fed
   With manna from above,
   And over is thy banner spread
   Of everlasting love.

6. He bids us drink and eat
   Imperishable food;
   He gives his flesh to be our meat,
   And bids us drink his blood.

7. What e'er the almighty can
   To pardoned sinners give,
   The fullness of our God made man
   We here with Christ receive.

19. Jesus – the name high over all

Easter ought really to be the chief festival of the Church. For many it is overtaken by Christmas and, for Christians in country areas, even by harvest. It is not an easy time of year, especially for those who are bereaved. Talk of sacrifice can seem gruesome and unhelpful. Resurrection can feel like an unkind and unrealistic hope.

Sometimes I let my mind wander in imagination. What were those first days of Easter like? Mingle with me amongst the crowds on Palm Sunday. Listen to the conversations. Children run to and fro. There is a sense of festival, of celebration, anticipation in the air. While the children play their games some of the adults reminisce. They'd walked this road before, remembered Passover, and held tightly to prophetic words which spoke of hope for them, for the world. The Torah was full of expectation, of a Messiah coming on the clouds in a chariot bringing judgement and liberation. Another theme presented an image of sensitive compassion, the picture of hands cupped around a smouldering wick, gently nurturing the dying embers till they came to flame again, or a horticulturalist tending a bruised reed so that it would heal and flourish.

A kingdom was pictured in which mercy and justice would flourish, where streams of living water would flow through a dry and barren desert, where dry bones would be clothed with flesh and leap, dancing back to life.

Among those people walking to Jerusalem were those who had been in a synagogue some three years before when a young Galilean preacher had rolled up a scroll and proclaimed that these words were coming true in that time, on that very day. The recollections merged with prophetic words and present experience: 'Rejoice greatly, O daughter Zion! Shout aloud, O daughter Jerusalem! Lo, your king comes to you;

triumphant and victorious is he, humble and riding on a donkey, on a colt, the foal of a donkey' (Zechariah 9.9).

In their eyes Jesus was that king.

1. Jesus – the name high over all,
   In hell, or earth, or sky!
   Angels and men before it fall,
   And devils fear and fly.

2. Jesus – the name to sinners dear,
   The name to sinners given!
   It scatters all their guilty fear,
   It turns their hell to heaven.

3. Jesus – the prisoner's fetters breaks,
   And bruises Satan's head;
   Power into strengthless souls it speaks,
   And life into the dead.

4. O that the world might taste and see
   The riches of his grace!
   The arms of love that compass me
   Would all mankind embrace.

5. His only righteousness I show,
   His saving grace proclaim;
   'Tis all my business here below
   To cry: 'Behold the Lamb!'

6. Happy if with my latest breath
   I might but gasp his name;
   Preach him to all, and cry in death:
   'Behold, behold the Lamb!'

20. Jesus, we follow thee

Imagine. It is Palm Sunday. We enter Jerusalem in the crowd with a feeling of expectation, a sense of triumph. The procession weaves its way to the Temple. Some people peel off on the way, renewing acquaintances, pausing to talk with friends they've not seen for a year or more. Others, in curiosity, join and walk along captivated by the throng, attracted by the waving of palm branches, hearing the laughter of children. Joy and excitement fill the air. Stall-holders ply their wares, street sellers call across the crowd, beggars reach with pleading hands and soulful eyes. All the sights, sounds and smells of the city are there. Still Jesus moves inexorably forward, and still we follow.

Now the Temple towers ahead of us. There is no slowing of pace, no quietening, no hush in expectation. In fact the voices of the people rise to a tumult. Psalms ring through their minds:

Who shall ascend the hill of the LORD? And who shall stand in his holy place?

Those who have clean hands and pure hearts, who do not lift up their souls to what is false, and do not swear deceitfully.

They will receive blessing from the LORD, and vindication from the God of their salvation.

(Psalm 24.3-5)

Jesus does not slacken his pace through the gates and into the courtyard. Only then does he stop, abruptly. He looks round.

Making a whip of cords, he drove all of them out of the temple, both the sheep and the cattle. He also poured out the coins of the money-changers and overturned their tables. He told those who were selling the doves, 'Take these things out of here! Stop making my Father's house a marketplace!'

(John 2.15-16)

Is it here, and is it now, at this point and in this place that they realize what is happening? And now, do we realize how costly discipleship can be?

1. Jesus, we follow thee,
   In all thy footsteps tread,
   And seek for full conformity
   To our exalted head.

2. We would, we would partake
   Thy every state below,
   And suffer all things for thy sake,
   And to thy glory go.

3. We in thy birth are born,
   Sustain thy grief and loss,
   Share in thy want, and shame, and scorn,
   And die upon the cross.

4. Baptized into thy death,
   We sink into thy grave,
   Till thou the quickening Spirit breathe,
   And to the utmost save.

5. Thou saidst, 'Where'er I am,
   There shall my servants be.'
   Master, thy welcome word we claim,
   And die to live with thee.

6. To us who share thy pain,
   Thy joy shall soon be given,
   And we shall in thy glory reign,
   For thou art now in heaven.

21. Victim divine, thy grace we claim

I wonder if you've ever signed an agreement and only afterwards realized what the small print meant? You make an insurance claim and find that you're not covered.

For disciples walking by the Sea of Galilee perhaps it was a bit like that. A slow dawning as the sun came up over the mountains shimmering across the sea making ripples erupt with flashes of reflected flame, mirrored in the gradual realization of the costliness of discipleship. Those days in Jerusalem were days of challenge and testing for those who thought themselves followers of Jesus. They heard him confronting teachers in the Temple. They questioned him and he gave as good as he got. Dangerous talk this, threatening authority and undermining vested interests. It is difficult to read these passages and then to say that Christianity doesn't have a political dimension. Here sacred and secular were immutably enmeshed. Challenge one and you undermine the other. Jesus felt the challenge himself. One account has him going to Bethany to 'recharge his batteries' before entering the thick of it all.

Then he ate with friends, received the betrayer's kiss. Judas hands over Jesus, the bargain has been struck.

But perhaps the real handing over had taken place 30 years before as God 'emptied himself of all but love' and put himself into the hands of human parents, at the whim of the political and religious powers of this world. The victim dips in the cup with the betrayer. The offering has begun: 'This is my body, my blood.' Bread and wine used as powerful symbols as Jesus shares that meal as 'priest and victim' of the eucharistic feast.

1. Victim divine, thy grace we claim,
   While thus thy precious death we show;
   Once offered up, a spotless lamb,
   In thy great temple here below,
   Thou didst for all mankind atone,
   And standest now before the throne.

2. Thou standest in the holiest place,
   As now for guilty sinners slain;
   Thy blood of sprinkling speaks, and prays,
   All-prevalent for helpless man;
   Thy blood is still our ransom found,
   And spreads salvation all around.

3. We need not now go up to heaven,
   To bring the long-sought Saviour down;
   Thou art to all already given,
   Thou dost ev'n now thy banquet crown:
   To every faithful soul appear,
   And show thy real presence here!

22. Christ, whose glory fills the skies

Children love Easter. All the images of new life, bunnies and Easter chicks and, of course, Easter eggs. A friend of mine reminded me that in Australia at the time that we celebrate Easter it is autumn. Leaves are becoming brightly coloured, fluttering down in the breeze or driven from the trees by fierce gales. Stark skeletons remain where once there was greenery. It challenges our familiar images. This time of Easter has been shrouded with seasonal pictures which cover the real canvas. Like an art restorer, we need to strip away the coated grime of centuries from the original painting and seek the meaning that lies beneath.

There is so much for us to celebrate. It shouldn't really surprise us that God could not be confined within a tomb, if this Jesus really is God. You cannot, in Sydney Carter's terms, cage the bird of heaven. God is greater than our capacity to contain or confine, or even to name or to define. So that's a start. Easter speaks of the incredible power of God.

Secondly, it speaks of the ultimate impossibility of erasing goodness from the world and from humanity. We live in an age where torture and terrorism seem to be forever in the media. It is easy to label people mindless or evil when such deeds are perpetrated. Yet often what shines through is an indomitable strength of goodness, so powerful that people reach through the horror and the carnage to forgive, and lives are rebuilt with greater, not lesser, purpose.

There is nothing in all creation that can take away God's love and that love is demonstrated supremely in the life, death and resurrection of Jesus. Easter speaks of transformation, new beginnings, steadfast, permanent love and the immensity of God. Flowers, eggs, bunnies and talk of new life and birth may all point to these truths but they are not, in themselves, the truths. Let us not lose hold of the facts by smothering them in all the other trappings. The facts mean much, much more.

1. Christ, whose glory fills the skies,
   Christ, the true, the only light,
   Sun of righteousness, arise,
   Triumph o'er the shades of night;
   Day-spring from on high, be near;
   Day-star, in my heart appear.

2. Dark and cheerless is the morn
   Unaccompanied by thee:
   Joyless is the day's return,
   Till thy mercy's beams I see,
   Till they inward light impart,
   Glad my eyes, and warm my heart.

3. Visit then this soul of mine;
   Pierce the gloom of sin and grief;
   Fill me, radiancy divine;
   Scatter all my unbelief;
   More and more thyself display,
   Shining to the perfect day.

23. All ye that seek the Lord who died

'It's not there!' We've all had those occasions when we've been looking for something, searched high and low, and then someone makes us look stupid by telling us that what we're hunting for isn't where we're looking. We should have known that it had been moved, put away, that it never really belonged there in the first place. It's different, though, when we go to put flowers on a grave on the Sunday after we've buried a loved one on the Friday. We expect the grave to be relatively untouched. The men may have tidied it a bit since the funeral, wreaths and bouquets placed in a neat fashion, but the grave should be more or less the same. Imagine the worst then; you come to the grave on the Sunday. The earth is piled up. The coffin has gone. The grave is empty. You do not immediately think of resurrection, surely?

When Mark the Evangelist wrote the story of that first Easter Sunday morning he got it right, I think. Look at it again. The women arrive early. The day before, the Sabbath, they couldn't come, but now they wanted to make things right. No flowers for them, but spices. They knew that the tomb in which Jesus had been placed was blocked by a heavy stone, like a millstone. To their consternation it had been rolled to one side, opening the grave. And the body was nowhere to be seen! No alleluias. The women flee in terror, in horror. Jesus has been taken and they don't know where or by whom. The author of John's Gospel writes of Mary Magdalene asking the gardener, 'Tell me where they have put my Lord.' The women, afraid of ridicule, tell no one what has happened. Only when Mary hears Jesus call her name does she recognize that he has been raised from the dead.

So resurrection is not nearly as obvious to those first disciples. Realistic, that: they needed repeated meetings to make sense of what had happened. The Early Church struggled to find purpose in Jesus' death. No wonder we still struggle with it today; and perhaps we shouldn't be so quick to ridicule those who find that belief difficult.

1. All ye that seek the Lord who died,
   Your God for sinners crucified,
   Now, now let all your grief be o'er!
   Believe, and ye shall weep no more.

2. The Lord of life is risen indeed,
   To death delivered in your stead;
   His rise proclaims your sins forgiven,
   And shows the living way to heaven.

3. Haste then, ye souls that first believe,
   Who dare the gospel word receive,
   Your faith with joyful hearts confess,
   Be bold, be Jesus' witnesses.

4. Go, tell the followers of your Lord
   Their Jesus is to life restored;
   He lives, that they his life may find;
   He lives to quicken all mankind.

24. Christ the Lord is risen today

I remember once seeing a painting of the ascending Christ. A group of men on a hillside stood with eyes upraised staring at a cloud. Two human feet were sticking out from the beneath the cloud. It looked faintly ridiculous. Ascension Day is on a Thursday each year and I know of untold preachers of stature who would rather not have to preach on this day or the Sunday near it. This is one Christian concept which seems to fly in the face of sense, so it's best to avoid it. But if we do that we miss something crucial to our Christianity. True, the picture that we have to go on is crudely painted but the truth that it represents is imperative to our belief and action.

To begin with, if God really did come to birth in the person of Jesus, if he grew to be a man, was, in the words of the Creed, 'crucified, dead and buried; raised on the third day', then we have a problem. If resurrection is real then, somehow, Jesus has to be removed from the frame without dying again. A crude, but simple, solution is ascension. Don't stop there though. Don't even go there if it doesn't help!

It has been critical to the survival of the Church, to the continuation of Jesus' teaching and values, for people to take those teachings and values on board, to live them and convey them from one generation to another. But there is no point to this if Jesus is still around, as he can go on doing the job. So for the perpetuation of his life, teaching and example the ascension, or something very like it, is essential.

Forget for a moment that crude painting; forget the manner of the ascension. Think of it this way: Jesus had taught the disciples. He had done all he could; time now for them to take over. Unless he goes they won't act. So he sends them away from him to Jerusalem where they are to wait until the Holy Spirit comes. What happens to him next is irrelevant to the story; we need not bother ourselves with it. What matters is the continuing narrative, the ongoing life, existence and witness of those people who are going to become the Church. Their life is our life. We pick up the responsibility where others left off. It was true then and it is true now. The celebration of ascension is the celebration of God's people coming of age, taking responsibility themselves to be as Christ in the world in every age and place.

1. Christ the Lord is risen today;
   Alleluia!
   Sons of men and angels say:
   Raise your joys and triumphs high;
   Sing, ye heavens; thou earth, reply:

2. Love's redeeming work is done,
   Fought the fight, the battle won;
   Vain the stone, the watch, the seal;
   Christ hath burst the gates of hell:

3. Vain the stone, the watch, the seal;
   Christ hath burst the gates of hell:
   Death in vain forbids his rise;
   Christ hath opened paradise.

4. Lives again our glorious king;
   Where, O death, is now thy sting?
   Once he died our souls to save;
   Where's thy victory, boasting grave?

5. Soar we now where Christ hath led,
   Following our exalted head;
   Made like him, like him we rise;
   Ours the cross, the grave, the skies:

6. King of glory! Soul of bliss!
   Everlasting life is this,
   Thee to know, thy power to prove,
   Thus to sing, and thus to love.

25. Jesus, we look to thee

Bereavement is awful. I know that is an understatement, and it sounds almost commonplace to say it. Yet there are times after someone has died when it can seem as though they are very near, for some people anyway. It feels more real than a dream and it isn't our imagination tricking us. This is reality and it's good. For most people it's a passing phase.

For the disciples it was, perhaps, no different. In one sense they felt that they had been bereaved twice. Jesus had been executed on the cross. Then logic had been confounded and he had walked among them, talked with them, ate with them. The disciples had felt that Jesus was really there but then he had dashed their hopes. He was going to leave them, and at the ascension St Matthew records that 'some doubted'. Perhaps it was like being orphaned all over again. There was just one thing, this promise of God's Spirit to be with them always. But just how real would that feel? It certainly became real enough to inspire and encourage and enliven the disciples. And so the Church began.

Now, today, as people worship Sunday by Sunday there is the hope, even the expectation that amidst our friends and relatives, Jesus will be there, that this will be a time of meeting the divine, of being in the real presence of God.

1. Jesus, we look to thee,
   Thy promised presence claim;
   Thou in the midst of us shalt be,
   Assembled in thy name.

2. Thy name salvation is,
   Which here we come to prove;
   Thy name is life and health and peace
   And everlasting love.

3. We meet, the grace to take
   Which thou hast freely given;
   We meet on earth for thy dear sake,
   That we may meet in heaven.

4. Present we know thou art,
   But O thyself reveal!
   Now, Lord, let every bounding heart
   The mighty comfort feel.

5. O may thy quickening voice
   The death of sin remove;
   And bid our inmost souls rejoice
   In hope of perfect love!

The conversion of John and Charles Wesley

26. Where shall my wondering soul begin?

Some people in the Church will always begin a conversation with a question, 'Are you saved?', it gives them an opportunity to begin to evangelize. Many are sincere but, however well meaning they are, I always feel like asking, 'Saved for what?' Christians believe that all people have gifts given by God. Part of our walk of discipleship is to find out what those gifts are and how we can best use them. Part of the responsibility of the Church is to help in that and then to encourage us and enable us.

When John and Charles Wesley were children they lived in the rectory in Epworth in Lincolnshire. Once there was a fire at the rectory and this left a persistent image on the memories of the members of the family. One detail in particular stayed with the brothers: Little Jackie, as John was known, was rescued from a bedroom window on the men's shoulders. The family interpreted this as a sign that John had been kept for a purpose. They said that he was a 'brand plucked from the burning', a quotation from Zechariah 3.2. From that point forward John's mother felt she had an obligation to him and to God to enable his growth in faith and his service of the Church.

As he grew up John, and indeed his brother Charles, found their gifts in preaching and writing, in building up the people of God in faith. They were willing to risk life and limb, as well as the derision of their friends, to achieve this end.

Many years ago I was talking about using our gifts in the Church to another minister. I complained about how there was so much else to do that seemed to prevent me from doing the things to which I really felt called. With wisdom he replied, 'Well, if you don't act, don't expect anyone else to, it's up to you.' It took a number of years to disentangle myself from the things I'd been doing to free the time and space to write. Now I have that space I'd better be sure to exercise the gift! And so far I've not had to take many risks.

So what is your purpose here? What have you been saved for? What have you to do for God and your neighbour? What are you willing to risk to follow that calling?

1. Where shall my wondering soul begin?
   How shall I all to heaven aspire?
   A slave redeemed from death and sin,
   A brand plucked from eternal fire,
   How shall I equal triumphs raise,
   Or sing my great deliverer's praise?

2. O how shall I the goodness tell,
   Father, which thou to me hast showed?
   That I, a child of wrath and hell,
   I should be called a child of God,
   Should know, should feel my sins forgiven,
   Blest with this antepast of heaven!

3. And shall I slight my Father's love?
   Or basely fear his gifts to own?
   Unmindful of his favours prove?
   Shall I, the hallowed cross to shun,
   Refuse his righteousness to impart
   By hiding it within my heart?

4. Outcasts of men, to you I call,
   Harlots, and publicans, and thieves!
   He spreads his arms to embrace you all;
   Sinners alone his grace receives:
   No need of him the righteous have;
   He came the lost to seek and save.

5. Come, O my guilty brethren, come,
   Groaning beneath your load of sin!
   His bleeding heart shall make you room,
   His open side shall take you in;
   He calls you now, invites you home:
   Come, O my guilty brethren, come!

27. And can it be

One of the most frightening jobs I can imagine is that of winchman on a rescue helicopter. There he is dangling on a line, suspended halfway between the orange chopper and the green-and-white crested sea. That line, his grip and skill and that of the pilot are all there are between life and death for the people on the tossing craft below. We watch in imagination as he is lowered. People below seem to be pleading, almost praying. The ship on which they are standing is pitching and tossing, rising and falling 20 or 30 feet at a time. Eventually the winchman finds a footing with them, puts on a harness. They are caught up, winched away, pulled to safety. Relief! There is no triumph here, not for them. They have been totally dependent on someone else risking their life on their behalf. Shivering with fear and cold they say words, none of which can be enough to frame their gratitude, 'Thank you.' And perhaps, later, saviour and saved share a drink together.

On 24 May 1738 John Wesley 'felt his heart strangely warmed'. Less well known, Charles Wesley, a few days before on Whit Sunday, had had a similar experience. Lying on what was feared would be his death bed in a mechanic's home, he sensed a voice telling him to rise and to believe. He was aware of the words from Isaiah 41.1, 'Comfort ye, my people'. He felt at peace with God. Some feel sure that it was this experience that led Charles to write the words, 'Where shall my wondering soul begin', others relate 'And can it be' to this time.

I remember, many years ago, being part of a small congregation. It was a service of Communion. I'd been there before and shared this sacrament, many times. We moved forward in turn. Knelt at the rail, held out our hands. The minister moved from person to person. Put ordinary bread into our hands one by one. Spoke quietly. Then the wine.

There was no great show, no spectacle. The building was plain, the ceremony simple. Then, all having received, some words of Scripture were said; I can't remember which, it doesn't matter. And we rose to our feet. Walked slowly, humbly away, back to our seats. The feeling was strange, mystical, overwhelming; the response one of awe-filled amazement, an immense awareness of the personal love of God. And you can explain all of this away. I could myself. I have been further from God before and since. But at that moment the sense of communion was complete. I have no doubt that a Muslim at the Hajj; a Jew at Passover might have the same sense of the nearness of God. This was my moment, singular, personal. I think Charles Wesley would have understood what I felt on that morning.

1. And can it be that I should gain
   An interest in the Saviour's blood?
   Died he for me, who caused his pain?
   For me, who him to death pursued?
   Amazing love! How can it be
   That thou, my God, shouldst die for me?

2. 'Tis mystery all: the Immortal dies!
   Who can explore his strange design?
   In vain the first-born seraph tries
   To sound the depths of love divine.
   'Tis mercy all! Let earth adore,
   Let angel minds enquire no more.

3. He left his Father's throne above –
   So free, so infinite his grace –
   Emptied himself of all but love,
   And bled for Adam's helpless race.
   'Tis mercy all, immense and free;
   For, O my God, it found out me!

4. Long my imprisoned spirit lay
   Fast bound in sin and nature's night;
   Thine eye diffused a quickening ray –
   I woke, the dungeon flamed with light,
   My chains fell off, my heart was free,
   I rose, went forth, and followed thee.

5. No condemnation now I dread;
   Jesus, and all in him, is mine!
   Alive in him, my living head,
   And clothed in righteousness divine,
   Bold I approach the eternal throne,
   And claim the crown, through Christ, my own.

28. My heart is full of Christ, and longs

Brilliant! I never thought it would be like that. You look back to that moment of revelation, that time of confirmation. You'd always hoped that something wonderful might happen some day, even to you. And this is that precious moment. You can't hold it in; you have to tell someone.

Time and again in the gospel story we find people, a cured leper, a woman at a well, who just could not keep a secret. They go off gossiping the gospel for all they're worth. I don't mean preaching either. These people had had their lives turned around and they had to say what had happened; they were full of it, they couldn't help bursting out with excitement. Oh yes, they looked foolish, I'm sure. People noticed them and asked what was going on. They couldn't help themselves. Who was it said, 'Preach the gospel, and if necessary use words'? They must have heard him!

When Charles Wesley found his life turned around by God, one of the things he couldn't do was to keep it to himself. His way of responding was by writing hymns, thousands of them. His brother rode thousands of miles on horse back, praying and preaching, driven by an inner force that compelled him, which he could not resist.

Neither let the message just rest in words. They visited condemned prisoners, spoke with the sick, encouraged and confirmed people in faith, and sought to abolish slavery. Their legacy spread throughout the world.

And today we need to give vent to that same sense of call. Has nothing good happened in your life? Is it not attributable to God? Of course, there may have been a human agent involved. John Wesley spoke with Peter Boehler, a German Moravian. Peter heard Jesus speak. You have heard a preacher, read your Bible, witnessed the self-giving of Gandhi or Mandela, Mother Teresa or Bob Geldof. But what are you going to do about it?

Recapture the excitement and tell people about it – for all you're worth!

1. My heart is full of Christ, and longs
   Its glorious matter to declare!
   Of him I make my loftier songs,
   I cannot from his praise forbear;
   My ready tongue makes haste to sing
   The glories of my heavenly king.

2. Fairer than all the earth-born race,
   Perfect in comeliness thou art;
   Replenished are thy lips with grace,
   And full of love thy tender heart:
   God ever blest! We bow the knee,
   And own all fullness dwells in thee.

3. Gird on thy thigh the Spirit's sword,
   And take to thee thy power divine;
   Stir up thy strength, almighty Lord,
   All power and majesty are thine:
   Assert thy worship and renown;
   O all-redeeming God, come down!

4. Come, and maintain thy righteous cause,
   And let thy glorious toil succeed;
   Dispread the victory of thy cross,
   Ride on, and prosper in thy deed;
   Through earth triumphantly ride one,
   And reign in every heart alone.

Pentecost

29. Spirit of truth, come down

As a lad I went to a traditional, old-fashioned boys' school. My eyesight wouldn't let me play football or cricket, and the sports I was best at were those where you just dug in and kept going. I used to cycle between 300-500 miles a week and I swam regularly. I once ran in the school cross-country team. One of our sports' teachers had been in the armed forces. He was renowned for being hard. I don't know how he would have survived in a school today. On a wet, slippery, muddy day, I came round the corner of the cross-country course, slid into a ditch and fell. Made a right mess of it. I scrambled to my feet while he watched. He said nothing. I clawed my way out and started to run again. I'd gone about a hundred yards when I heard his voice carrying on the wind, 'That's the spirit!' It made all the difference.

I imagine God saying the same thing to us sometimes. When we've had a hard day and, nevertheless, we do what we need to do I imagine God saying, 'That's the spirit!' When, through the tireless action of aid agencies children are fed and homeless people housed, 'That's the spirit!' When we visit a neighbour or care for a relative, 'That's the spirit!' The point is that the Spirit, the Holy Spirit, is that gift of God that helps us to behave as Jesus would if he were here today. The Spirit allows God to be active in the world today. Nothing mystical in that. No strange words or foreign tongues, no shouting or raising our hands in the air, no loud singing; just the simple, tenacious, persistent love of God permeating each action that we do and each word that we say: 'That's the spirit!'

So at Pentecost, when we celebrate the Holy Spirit coming to the first disciples, remember that the outflowing of that Spirit resulted in a practical transformation of Jesus' disciples. It gave them the courage and conviction that enabled them to share all their possessions, to worship, to care for each other and to meet for meals with a sense of abundant celebration and joy. Wherever they went the world was a better place for their presence.

We may use theological language, talk of salvation or anointing, but it is the living, active faith that is the best witness to the presence of God. Without it our celebrations and protestations are empty. With it, well, 'That's the spirit!'

1. Spirit of truth, come down,
   Reveal the things of God;
   And make to us salvation known,
   And witness with the blood.

2. No man can truly say
   That Jesus is the Lord
   Unless thou take the veil away,
   And breathe the living Word.

3. Then, only then, we feel
   Our interest in his blood,
   And cry with joy unspeakable,
   Thou art my Lord, my God!

4. O that we now might know
   The all-atoning Lamb!
   Spirit of faith, descend and show
   The virtue of his name.

5. Inspire the living faith,
   Which whosoe'er receives,
   The witness in himself he hath,
   And savingly believes.

30. O thou who camest from above

One of the problems that the Church has faced over the years is how to deal with its paid employees. 'A workman is worthy of his hire' is bandied about but then there are those who would remind us that grace is free and we shouldn't have to pay to hear the gospel and those who preach it should do it for love of God. Well, there's a can of worms to open up!

Jesus spoke of it being meat and drink to do the will of God until it was complete. Well, that answers it. We need to feed to stay alive, so as long as we are alive we should do God's will. That's clear. But this is a definition of a Christian. Someone who works for the Church may well be a Christian and his or her discipleship will never end while they are alive. A particular job probably will come to an end. The distinction is important. If the employees of the Church are worked into the ground, the employers are culpable! Well, then, I've got that off my chest!

As for our Christian calling, that discipleship, being a learner of Jesus – for that's what it means – we are on a life-long contract. Jeremiah spoke of a fire burning in his bones, Richard Rolle, the fourteenth-century mystic, spoke of the 'Fire of Love', John Wesley's heart was 'strangely warmed'. And if the fire is kindled in us it should never go out. This is no short-term commitment, no flash in the pan, so pray carefully, if you will, 'kindle a flame of sacred love on the mean altar of my heart ... till death thy endless mercies seal'!

1. O thou who camest from above
   The pure celestial fire to impart,
   Kindle a flame of sacred love
   On the mean altar of my heart!

2. There let it for thy glory burn
   With inextinguishable blaze,
   And trembling to its source return,
   In humble prayer and fervent praise.

3. Jesus, confirm my heart's desire
   To work, and speak, and think for thee;
   Still let me guard the holy fire,
   And still stir up thy gift in me.

4. Ready for all thy perfect will,
   My acts of faith and love repeat,
   Till death thy endless mercies seal,
   And make the sacrifice complete.

Trinity

31. Young men and maidens, raise

I live in a part of the world where old traditions, mummer's plays and May festivals still take place; a part of old England with Morris Dancers, not drum majorettes or cheer-leaders, but men and women with bells, hankies, a drum and accordion. Picturesque, entertaining, nostalgic; and I imagine a May festival from very long ago. The winter is past, the crops are growing, and summer and harvest are promised, waiting in the wings. For a brief time there is a lull in the rhythm of the life of the countryside, time for joy and merrymaking.

So many Christian festivals have their origins way back before the time of Jesus and traditional celebrations evolve constantly, gaining new levels of meaning and significance. An eighteenth-century clergyman, not known for merrymaking, his brother less so, looks out on a village scene. The scales drop from puritanical eyes and he is carried away in the joy of the moment. He watches young men and women reel about, first this way then that, the music tuning their steps. Laughter fills the air and the enjoyment had a rustic purity about it. The muse begins to rise in him; he heads indoors, takes pen and paper and begins to write. It is the season of Trinity. Ascension and Pentecost are past and the Church pauses to assess, to reaffirm its belief. Well, why not bring a bit of joy to the proceedings? A smile wins more souls than a frown!

1. Young men and maidens, raise
   Your tuneful voices high;
   Old men and children, praise
   The Lord and earth and sky:
       Him three in one, and one in three,
       Extol to all eternity!

2. The universal king
   Let all the world proclaim;
   Let every creature sing
   His attributes and name!
       Chorus

3. In his great name alone
   All excellencies meet,
   Who sits upon the throne,
   And shall for ever sit:
       Chorus

4. Glory to God belongs.
   Glory to God be given,
   Above the noblest songs
   Of all in earth or heaven!
       Chorus

32. Jesus, the gift divine I know

Days of spring, May Days of the past with their dancing and celebration were not unlike the great Christian celebrations that we see from time to time today, the annual gatherings to which people flock. At their best these meetings confirm or deepen faith and reassure us that we are not on our own as we seek to follow Jesus, to live lives like his. May Day celebrations pass and life goes back to normal. We've had a good time. But for the Christian life never 'goes back to normal', it is always the counter-cultural witness of poverty in the face of riches, justice in the face of deceit, mercy offered over against condemnation. The celebration week or weekend can sometimes take us so far away from that reality that in the fun and joy we lose sight of our true calling. We sing the songs, dance the dance and remain oblivious to the call of God. It is all too much fun and we'd rather it didn't stop.

Joy is valid. It is a gift of God. But the truth is that human happiness can be finite. The gifts of God, in contrast, have an eternal dimension and it is these gifts that help us to go on when the superficial praise has lost its shine, when we are back amid the humdrum, everyday pressures of living our lives.

Charles Wesley's goal was to have the mind, the spirit of Christ within him. That can bring joy; it is not a selfish aim but one which, he envisages, will help him in meeting the needs of orphans, widows, the poor, those who suffer. In them he saw the Christ he sought to love, and when this happens it is a divine gift indeed!

Wesley did not want second best and neither should we!

1. Jesus, the gift divine I know,
   The gift divine I ask of thee;
   That living water now bestow –
   Thy Spirit and thyself, on me;
   Thou, Lord, of life the fountain art;
   Now let me find thee in my heart.

2. Thee let me drink, and thirst no more
   For drops of finite happiness;
   Spring up, O Well, in heavenly power,
   In streams of pure perennial peace,
   In joy that none can take away,
   In life which shall for ever stay.

3. Father, on me the grace bestow,
   Unblamable before thy sight,
   Whence all the streams of mercy flow;
   Mercy, thine own supreme delight,
   To me, for Jesus' sake, impart,
   And plant thy nature in my heart.

4. Thy mind throughout my life be shown,
   While, listening to the sufferer's cry,
   The widow's and the orphan's groan,
   On mercy's wings I swiftly fly,
   The poor and helpless to relieve,
   My life, my all, for them to give.

5. Thus may I show thy Spir't within,
   Which purges me from every stain;
   Unspotted from the world and sin,
   My faith's integrity maintain;
   The truth of my religion prove
   By perfect purity and love.

33. Hail! Holy, holy, holy Lord!

A friend of mine once said that he could only believe in a God that he could understand. And then made the obvious statement that a God he could understand would be no God.

People have struggled for centuries to make sense of God. We are no different. Sometimes people have been so sure of what they believed God to be like that they have fought wars over it. Metaphors, pictures used to describe God, have been regarded as reality, unchangeable and beyond contradiction. Yet they are only ever pictures, no more real than the photo of a favourite aunt is that favourite aunt. As for God, God is beyond description or understanding.

I began my walk of faith with a belief in some power behind creation. There was such wonder in a sunset or the stark skeleton of a tree shorn of leaves in winter. It went beyond what I could understand or explain scientifically.

Then as I read the Bible I began to feel that the person who we know as Jesus really was incredibly special. But the incredible is literally unbelievable, and I could believe in Jesus. The picture we have of him is credible as a picture of a human being. His behaviour as a child I see mirrored in children all around me. He was not unlike children I taught in school. As a man he had the capacity to think on his feet, to argue and persuade. Sometimes he must have been hard to live with, seemingly contradictory, always loving. And he died a human death. Don't mask that. It was real.

Looking around me I sometimes find myself startled by immense generosity, incredible self-sacrifice. There is much love in the world if we are open to it. And when I see hungry children being fed or people struggling against all odds to help each other rebuild homes after a tsunami or earthquake, when I see old soldiers meeting and grasping hands, exchanging stories and memories of times when they were sworn enemies, I sense something of the spirit of Jesus still alive in the world.

The Trinity is just a picture. Not something I'd die for, not something I'd even argue for that strongly. But it's a good picture, and it helps us to understand the continuing creativity, passion, generosity and presence of the God we worship. So I'll not deride it. I'll use the picture carefully; and not get it out of perspective, I hope!

1. Hail! Holy, holy, holy Lord!
   Whom One in Three we know;
   By all thy heavenly host adored,
   By all thy church below.

2. One undivided Trinity
   With triumph we proclaim;
   Thy universe is full of thee,
   And speaks thy glorious name.

3. Thee, holy Father, we confess,
   Thee, holy Son, adore,
   Thee, Spir't of truth and holiness,
   We worship evermore.

4. Three Persons equally divine
   We magnify and love;
   And both the choirs ere long shall join
   To sing thy praise above:

5. Hail! Holy, holy, holy Lord,
   Our heavenly song shall be,
   Supreme, essential One, adored
   In co-eternal Three.

The Body of Christ

34. Christ, from whom all blessings flow

It's hard not to be moved by the way in which people who have shared a devastating experience find themselves feeling closer to one another than they do to members of their families. After all, only they know what they've been through. Theirs is a bond which can never be dissolved. There is a great temptation to try to form such a bond between people. The longing after a sense of community in which we care for one another and no one is left out is, perhaps, one such symptom of this. It is given expression in clubs, organizations, religious orders and trade unions. Not least is this seen in the Church. There is a hankering after that supposed ideal world, born out of hardship, that is pictured in Acts 2 where the believers held everything in common and there seemed to be a sense of harmonious agreement, however short-lived, between them.

John and Charles Wesley sought after something of this sort in the Holy Club in Oxford and afterwards in the Methodist Societies that they began to form. Here people could be open with one another and they were encouraged to build each other up, to think of each other's needs.

At its best the Church is a body of people in which no one is excluded and in which those things which humanly separate us are swept away by God's love for us and our love for each other. Here 'Names, and sects, and parties fall' as women and men are bound more closely to each other in commitment and fellowship. Here is a vision of what the world could be.

1. Christ, from whom all blessings flow,
   Perfecting the saints below,
   Hear us, who thy nature share,
   Who thy mystic body are.

2. Join us, in one spirit join,
   Let us still receive of thine;
   Still for more on thee we call,
   Thou who fillest all in all.

3. Closer knit to thee, our Head,
   Nourished, Lord, by thee, and fed,
   Let us daily growth receive,
   More in Jesus Christ believe.

4. Never from thy service move,
   Needful to each other prove,
   Use the grace on each bestowed,
   Tempered by the art of God.

5. Love, like death, has all destroyed,
   Rendered all distinctions void;
   Names, and sects, and parties fall:
   Thou, O Christ, art all in all.

35. And are we yet alive

For many families these days it takes a wedding, perhaps a christening or a funeral to bring everyone together. Listen on the edge of the crowd of this imaginary family for a moment. A teenager is greeted with 'My, how you've grown!' and moves off sheepishly blushing. Two elderly men are reminiscing about the old days. It's not all romantic rose-coloured spectacles; they remember the heartache and hazard, hardship and longing of those days. But the days were precious, some of the richest of their lives and they'll never come again. They glance across the room and remember the woman that one loved and another married and think on how it has been and might have been. Three women think of children and grandchildren and weddings past and time lost. A ripple of laughter crosses the room; tears are dried. Inevitably they remember, while the children play.

This family has come together again for another occasion. Some have survived, some have died. There has been illness and death, perhaps divorce, celebrations and birthdays, successes and joys. Here they meet again.

Every year the Conference of the Methodist Church begins with just such a remembrance. In a large hall or in a university or in the body of a church people gather for business. Greetings are exchanged. There's a lot of catching up to do. People wave and get one another's attention. Recollections are aired. The place is new and it is compared with the previous venue: the comfort of the seats, the air conditioning or lack of it.

Then there is a hush. The President of the Conference rises and before anything else at all we sing. And in the singing there is that recollection, so human, that pause to look around, to remember and to give thanks, to know that the love of God has seen us through and brought us together once more, and we wonder at it, 'And are we yet alive and see each other's face?' Always, always this hymn.

1. And are we yet alive,
   And see each other's face?
   Glory and praise to Jesus give
   For his redeeming grace!

2. Preserved by power divine
   To full salvation here,
   Again in Jesu's praise we join,
   And in his sight appear.

3. What troubles have we seen,
   What conflicts have we passed,
   Fightings without, and fears within,
   Since we assembled last!

4. But out of all the Lord
   Hath brought us by his love;
   And still he doth his help afford,
   And hides our life above.

5. Then let us make our boast
   Of his redeeming power,
   Which saves us to the uttermost,
   Till we can sin no more.

6. Let us take up the cross,
   Till we the crown obtain;
   And gladly reckon all things loss,
   So we may Jesus gain.

   > Praise ye the Lord, alleluia!
   > Praise ye the Lord, alleluia!
   > Alleluia, alleluia, alleluia,
   > Praise ye the Lord!

36. Captain of Israel's host, and guide

Who knows what the future will hold? We have no idea. That can sometimes be quite frightening if we dwell on it. And sometimes the fear is well-founded. The crew of a lifeboat would never go to sea if they thought what lay ahead. It is all too awful to contemplate. Anxiety about the unknown can be literally crippling.

At times like these remembering the past can help and not just our own past. One of the strengths of Judaism is the way in which year on year, season on season the acts of God are recalled. These events are not just memories of some divine whim acting in isolation. In each and every case the actions of God are related to the needs and security of the people. The most significant of these stories is that of the Exodus. A people in slavery are recognized by God and led to freedom against all the odds. Eventually they arrive in a Promised Land. Although the Exodus narrative has caused difficulty throughout history, as the people of Israel have claimed rights over territory and others have felt oppressed by that claim, there is a deep metaphorical truth underlying this story. God takes care of people and rescues them. People are safe with God whatever may befall. The image of wandering through a desert seeking a place to rest is powerful and evocative, and oppressed peoples have found comfort in this story in successive generations.

Each year as the Methodist Conference ends and people prepare to depart they relive something of that sense of exodus, if on a very small scale. Decisions have been made prayerfully and hopefully. Now is the time to return home yet also to leave friends. There is an expectation of meeting again in another year in another place, and now a claim is made, 'We shall not in the desert stray', 'We shall not full direction need', for 'love, almighty love, is near'. That love *is* always near and so as we set off on our life's journeys again there is a constant reminder in these words of the powerful, abiding presence of a God who will never leave us or forsake us. In this God we can trust.

1. Captain of Israel's host, and guide
   Of all who seek the land above,
   Beneath thy shadow we abide,
   The cloud of thy protecting love;
   Our strength, thy grace; our rule, thy word;
   Our end, the glory of the Lord.

2. By thine unerring Spirit led,
   We shall not in the desert stray;
   We shall not full direction need,
   Nor miss our providential way;
   As far from danger as from fear,
   While love, almighty love, is near.

Transfiguration

37. Jesus, let all thy lovers shine

Respite, that's what I need, respite. Do you ever have one of those periods when you just need lifting out of yourself? And then it comes, like a gift from God. You get an unexpected phone call, a letter, perhaps an e-mail from halfway across the globe. Suddenly your life is alight with unexpected joy and you want to cry out, 'Alleluia!' – Maybe you're too reserved. But no one's looking so you do it anyway, and take a little dance across the living room. Quick check... no one saw, it's all right! That was a heaven-sent pick me up, and now you can go on.

I've often thought that the story of the transfiguration was a bit like that. It's the middle of Jesus' ministry. We know that the story is moving him nearer to Jerusalem, to his trial and his death. Let's step back a bit. The disciples have been with him for some time now. They are travelling. They are tired. The crowds make demands. They need a rest. They set off for the hills and Jesus makes for the highest peak in the region. I don't know if you've been into the mountains but sometimes it's difficult to tell mist from low cloud. I remember once in North Wales seeing a cloud touch down on a mountain and lift off again leaving a covering of snow behind. It was mysterious, magnificent. Anyway, Jesus disappears into such a cloud. Wonderful, but not mystical. Then the disciples seem to see other figures there with him – Moses, Elijah – and Peter offers to make shelters for them. A voice is heard, 'This is my son, my beloved.' It is an echo of Jesus' baptism. A reaffirmation of his place, his person. A time of strengthening and reassurance, of exaltation and joy. Then the cloud disappears and the disciples are challenged about what they have seen, as to who Jesus is. Peter recognizes the Messiah but is told to keep it to himself. Only now can Jesus remind them that, yes, he really is going to suffer. As Peter protests, he is challenged and they make their way back to the plain, to people, to life, to service and the road to the cross; empowered.

We need a moment of transfiguration from time to time, not to escape, but to reassure, to give us spiritual rest and energy for the rest of life's journey. Then we can go on, back into the hurly-burly. And as Jesus went with the disciples back to the business of the plain and the road to Jerusalem, so God is with us in our continuing pilgrimage. We are not alone. We share a spark of divine glory and we can shine with the light of God.

1. Jesus, let all thy lovers shine
   Illustrious as the sun:
   And, bright with borrowed rays divine,
   Their glorious circuit run.

2. Beyond the reach of mortals, spread
   Their light where'er they go;
   And heavenly influences shed
   On all the world below.

3. As the bright Sun of Righteousness,
   Their healing wings display;
   And let their lustre still increase
   Unto the perfect day.

Summer days

38. Love divine, all loves excelling

If you are reading this book through, week by week, from the beginning of the year, a hymn a week, you are now well into the wedding season. Not that you can't get married at other times but summer still seems to be the most popular.

Look around many people's houses and on the walls or a sideboard there are photos. Among them, usually, is a wedding. Sometimes in black and white, inevitably outdated, these images can inspire a wry smile or a tear. Memories encapsulated, frozen.

One church where I was minister used to get a red carpet out for weddings. It reached from the church door down to the road. Every wedding felt like a right royal occasion and the stewards and organists treated it like that too. At another church the organist would come out at his own expense and play through anything the bride and groom thought they might like. And if inspiration was at a low ebb he'd graciously suggest something that he thought might be appropriate for them. Spare a thought for the organists on these occasions, struggling with Widor's *Toccata* or trying to play the groom's favourite tune never heard before on such an instrument. I once remember an older organist ending up putting in pedal notes against the melody that a rock guitarist friend of the bride and groom was playing. His only word at the end of the ceremony, quietly, just for my hearing was, 'Different'!

Spring and summer, times for best suits and dresses and bridesmaids, the chapel decked with flowers, the bride's mother with tears of joy, or regret? Everyone is moved by the emotion of the occasion.

Well, what do you sing for such a time of celebration? I guess that 'Love divine, all loves excelling' is sung more than anything else, either to Stainer's lovely, simple melody, or to 'the Welsh tune', as though there was only one Welsh tune, 'Blaenwern'.

But look at the words. John Wesley wouldn't even have the second verse his brother had written. It's said that he didn't like the idea of asking God to 'Take away our power of sinning'! As to the rest, the technical term is eschatological. The words point through and beyond this life until we are 'changed from glory into glory, till in heaven we take our place'. I guess that is not foremost in the minds of most couples as they stand before the minister! But what a thought: love that goes on and on and on without ending, till you meet God face to face. Glory indeed!

1. Love divine, all loves excelling,
   Joy of heaven to earth come down,
   Fix in us thy humble dwelling,
   All thy faithful mercies crown.
   Jesus, thou art all compassion
   Pure, unbounded love thou art;
   Visit us with thy salvation,
   Enter every trembling heart.

2. Breathe, O breathe thy loving Spirit
   Into every troubled breast,
   Let us all in thee inherit,
   Let us find that second rest;
   Take away our power of sinning,
   Alpha and Omega be,
   End of faith, as its beginning,
   Set our hearts at liberty.

3. Come, almighty to deliver,
   Let us all thy grace receive;
   Suddenly return, and never,
   Never more thy temples leave.
   Thee we would be always blessing,
   Serve thee as thy hosts above,
   Pray, and praise thee, without ceasing,
   Glory in thy perfect love.

4. Finish then thy new creation,
   Pure and spotless let us be;
   Let us see thy great salvation,
   Perfectly restored in thee:
   Changed from glory into glory,
   Till in heaven we take our place,
   Till we cast our crowns before thee,
   Lost in wonder, love, and praise!

39. Thou God of truth and love

It's amazing sometimes, isn't it, how we find ourselves placed alongside someone who needs us or whom we need? Just today I had an e-mail which caught me not only on the right day but at just the right time, from an old friend I'd almost forgotten, passing on the words of a prayer from across the globe. It doesn't matter what the words were, just that they were appropriate at that very moment.

People change jobs and houses much more than they used to in my childhood. Uprooting and setting down in a new place is one of the stress criteria they tell us. But it happens. And though it seems so random at the time, we meet and make new friends, colleagues, aquaintances, perhaps even a future partner. Charles Wesley moved about quite a bit – though not as much as his brother John – and meeting people and getting to know them raised a question for him:

> Why hast thou cast our lot
> In the same age and place,
> And why together brought
> To see each other's face ...

He answers it in the same breath: 'To join with loving sympathy, and mix our friendly souls in thee'. There is something of the human and the divine in each and every meeting. In a new office, Wesley would say, here is someone to befriend, with whom to empathize for he, like you, is a unique child of God. This neighbour who has made you your first cup of tea as the van unloads your belongings should be as Christ to you. There is, for Wesley, a divine purpose in every meeting. And you don't have to be fatalistic and think of God as working our every move as if we were just cogs in some giant cosmic machine, to grasp this. For Wesley everyone was a potential neighbour, he could see Christ in others and knew that they should be able to look for Christ in him. That's the essence of it.

And it's no wonder that for many of those who know this hymn, it's another favourite for weddings. Two people have their lot cast in the same age and place, brought together, made one, to travel on together with mutual care, seeking always to do God's will from beginning to end. Not a bad sentiment that, for two people sharing their lives together.

1. Thou God of truth and love
   We seek thy perfect way,
   Ready thy choice to approve,
   Thy providence to obey;
   Enter into thy wise design,
   And sweetly lose our will in thine.

2. Why hast thou cast our lot
   In the same age and place,
   And why together brought
   To see each other's face,
   To join with loving sympathy,
   And mix our friendly souls in thee?

3. Didst thou not make us one,
   That we might one remain,
   Together travel on,
   And share our joy and pain,
   Till all thy utmost goodness prove,
   And rise renewed in perfect love?

4. Then let us ever bear
   The blessèd end in view,
   And join, with mutual care,
   To fight our passage through;
   And kindly help each other on,
   Till all receive the starry crown.

5. O may thy Spirit seal
   Our souls unto that day,
   With all thy fullness fill,
   And then transport away:
   Away to our eternal rest,
   Away to our Redeemer's breast.

40. Open, Lord, my inward ear

Summer draws on and we seek relaxation and quiet. I remember times by the seaside or by quiet lakes. I love water, the ebb and flow of tides, the rush of moorland streams. If only I can get away from the crowds I can think, be at one with God. I remember as a teenager climbing to a rocky crag that overlooked my home town of Torquay. It wasn't a posh part of town; nearby was a sawmill. I'd climb to the height and then sit quietly looking out over the tiled roofs, watching the occasional gull swoop below me. Tranquillity.

Now, as an adult, I still sometimes crave that same solitude. Solitude isn't loneliness. It is a sense of being at one with nature and with God and having sufficient time just to reflect on all that is around us: to sit and simply watch a sunset, the changing colours, the differing light and the lengthening shadows, or to listen to the dawn chorus in a patch of woodland, distinguishing different voices as the birds wake from the night.

Then, once in a while, we have enough space to hear the voice of God. No, don't get me wrong, I'm not talking about voices which command me to do this or that, but the still, small voice in my head, the feeling that gives purpose and direction, the calm that gives a sense of peace in a world of constant rush and hurry.

I wonder if that is what Charles Wesley craved when he prayed, 'Open, Lord, my inward ear'. He spoke of a sense of rejoicing but also of a quiet heart, of withdrawing from a hurrying world. Then in the presence of God there was time to understand, to be at one with God in a quite mystical way, to recharge his faith. And there still is.

1. Open, Lord, my inward ear,
   And bid my heart rejoice;
   Bid my quiet spirit hear
   Thy comfortable voice;
   Never in the whirlwind found,
   Or where earthquakes rock the place,
   Still and silent is the sound,
   The whisper of thy grace.

2. From the world of sin, and noise,
   And hurry I withdraw;
   For the small and inward voice
   I wait with humble awe;
   Silent am I now and still,
   Dare not in thy presence move;
   To my waiting soul reveal
   The secret of thy love.

3. Thou didst undertake for me,
   For me to death wast sold;
   Wisdom in a mystery
   Of bleeding love unfold;
   Teach the lesson of thy cross:
   Let me die, with thee to reign;
   All things let me count but loss,
   So I may thee regain.

4. Show me, as my soul can bear,
   The depth of inbred sin;
   All the unbelief declare,
   The pride that lurks within;
   Take me, whom thyself hast bought,
   Bring into captivity
   Every high aspiring thought
   That would not stoop to thee.

5. Lord, my time is in thy hand,
   My soul to thee convert;
   Thou canst make me understand,
   Though I am slow of heart;
   Thine in whom I live and move,
   Thine the work, the praise is thine;
   Thou art wisdom, power, and love,
   And all thou art is mine.

41. God of all power, and truth, and grace

You know what it's like when you've been going down a particular road the same way for years and all of a sudden 'they' change it. Another one-way street! Even worse if you make your discovery when the policeman stops you half-way up going the wrong way!

Decimal money appears. I don't understand the electrics of my car any more. And my computer is out of date before I've got it out of the shop! Sometimes it's change for change's sake, sometimes there is real advance and we all benefit. Every time there is a change we have to adjust to it.

Then there are changes in the world: the catastrophic tumult of an earthquake or tsunami, leaving people homeless, all their belongings destroyed or swept away. People die as a consequence of illness or so-called natural causes which don't feel natural at all. 'Change and decay in all around I see' as the hymn puts it.

There are times when I wonder if I can manage another change, then when I go to church I find that even the stories of Jesus are not what I thought they were. I know logically that I need to learn and grow, however old I get, but I'm tempted to say, 'Is nothing sacred?' and reel off that text, 'Jesus, the same yesterday, today and forever'. I know that is true, but how I see Jesus, what I understand about Jesus has to change. I have more knowledge and understand more than I did when I was a child. I know what love and broken love is about. I've seen death and birth. I've watched my father come home redundant and then pick himself up. I know that life is not all security and comfort.

Then I sing this hymn. There are some things that are so much easier to believe if I sing them rather than read them or say them. Behind all the Bible stories is a God who shall 'from age to age endure'. Bring on the changes. Without some change I'll never get there!

1. God of all power, and truth, and grace,
   Which shall from age to age endure,
   Whose word, when heaven and earth shall pass,
   Remains and stands for ever sure;

2. That I thy mercy may proclaim,
   That all mankind thy truth may see,
   Hallow thy great and glorious name,
   And perfect holiness in me.

3. Thy sanctifying Spirit pour
   To quench my thirst and make me clean;
   Now, Father, let the gracious shower
   Descend, and make me pure from sin.

4. Give me a new, a perfect heart,
   From doubt, and fear, and sorrow free;
   The mind which was in Christ impart,
   And let my spirit cleave to thee.

5. O that I now, from sin released,
   Thy word may to the utmost prove,
   Enter into the promised rest,
   The Canaan of thy perfect love!

6. Now let me gain perfection's height,
   Now let me into nothing fall,
   Be less than nothing in thy sight,
   And feel that Christ is all in all.

A covenant relationship

42. All praise to our redeeming Lord

At the turn of the year Methodists renew their covenant, their promises with God.

Oh, hold on a minute. If you're reading this book through the year you might wonder what perverse choice has put this hymn here. Well, yes it is perverse. John Wesley once called the Methodists 'a peculiar people'. I don't think he meant strange, just different. Methodists begin their year not on 1 January or 5 April or even at the beginning of Advent but on the first day of September. Some churches still have their Covenant Service then.

It's a little like renewing baptismal or confirmation vows. It's a reminder of all we ought to be committed to as Christians but also of God's incredible, unfailing, steadfast love towards us. And the vows are made easier, indeed are perhaps only possible, in the light of that love. It is as though we are saying, 'I'll do anything for you, Daddy or Mummy'; and then our parent replies, 'I know, child, and I will do anything for you and I ask of you no more than you are really able because I love you as myself.'

Often this next hymn will be sung. As we contemplate doing all we can for God we recognize that that means that we do it for each other. It also means, if we're honest, that we need just a little bit of help from our friends. We recognize that God calls us to work as one and to build one another up. We mix together and, praise God, sometimes even agree with one another! It is a right and realistic goal to have set before us even if humanly we rarely achieve it.

No wonder it has become the chief hymn to be used in Lovefeasts – a sharing of food and drink in fellowship, not unlike Communion but not strictly a Communion service.

Lovefeasts are very informal and I imagine that mix of solemnity and joy that is perhaps associated with Passover.

So we go on hand in hand. And it is that line, and perhaps the whole tenor of the hymn, that has again led this to be seen as a wedding hymn. There is even some suggestion that Charles wrote it for his own wedding. What a mixture of possibilities and what a lovely tune we have in 'Julius'.

1. All praise to our redeeming Lord,
   Who joins us by his grace,
   And bids us, each to each restored,
   Together seek his face.

2. He bids us build each other up;
   And, gathered into one,
   To our high calling's glorious hope
   We hand in hand go on.

3. The gift which he on one bestows,
   We all delight to prove;
   The grace through every vessel flows,
   In purest streams of love.

4. Ev'n now we think and speak the same,
   And cordially agree;
   Concentred all, through Jesu's name,
   In perfect harmony.

5. We all partake the joy of one,
   The common peace we feel,
   A peace to sensual minds unknown,
   A joy unspeakable.

6. And if our fellowship below
   In Jesus be so sweet,
   What heights of rapture shall we know
   When round his throne we meet!

43. What shall I do my God to love

In 1953 the publisher Victor Gollancz wrote the second volume of his autobiography, *More for Timothy*. I had enjoyed the first volume, which I'd picked up second-hand; I do love second-hand bookshops. Anyway, I turned eagerly to this second volume. I opened it with anticipation. Gollancz had a way with words that as a writer I admired. Just nine lines in I froze and wept. I think he had probably done the same thing as he had written. These opening lines offer a vivid description of a man caught by napalm, his body so badly burned that he could neither sit nor lie down. The author looked up from his script, I imagine, and began to paint a word picture of his orchard. Confronted with such horror we are compelled to look, to stare, yet we simultaneously want to look away. Somehow we need to cope with the sense of grief and pain that we feel just looking at another's misery. And one way is to do something about it, if we can.

When Jesus met a leper (Mark 1.40–45) we are told that he was moved with pity (or in some translations compassion). The Greek word suggests a mixture of attraction and revulsion.

That was how I felt reading about this man, but what if I had been there? Jesus, meeting the leper, was attracted to him but it would have been so natural to turn away. As we read the story we find Jesus reaching out and touching the man. His feeling ran deep because he saw the physical plight of the man, and he also knew about his alienation from his community and religion. That alienation had to be challenged and changed. It began with the touch of a hand, of Jesus becoming one with him. It concluded when the man got the certificate from the priest showing that he was clean and allowing him to be part of society once more.

We are called to mirror this act of compassion, allowing our feelings to motivate us to act with and for those who are maimed or sick, homeless or alienated. This is where Charles Wesley begins as he reflects:

> What shall I do my God to love,
> My Saviour, and the world's, to praise?
> Whose bowels of compassion move
> To me and all the fallen race ...

That's a bit earthy for us, but the sense of our guts being knotted up at what we see is far closer to Scripture and reality than the softer words we find more comfortable to sing!

1. What shall I do my God to love,
   My Saviour, and the world's, to praise?
   Whose tenderest compassions move
   To me and all the fallen race,
   Whose mercy is divinely free
   For all the fallen race, and me!

2. I long to know, and to make known,
   The heights and depths of love divine,
   The kindness thou to me hast shown,
   Whose every sin was counted thine:
   My God for me resigned his breath;
   He died to save my soul from death.

3. How shall I thank thee for the grace
   On me and all mankind bestowed?
   O that my every breath were praise!
   O that my heart were filled with God!
   My heart would then with love o'erflow,
   And all my life thy glory show.

44. Jesus, Lord, we look to thee

For centuries nations have made war on nations. We're only human after all. We're told that our genes are selfish and that it's natural to fight for self-preservation.

It all began when we were animals drinking at the water hole, simultaneously watching our backs in case some predator made us part of his food chain. Then for our safety we gathered together, so that if we were attacked only those on the fringe of the herd died. Those at the centre survive. The next step was to take possession of the land, to make it ours. But our population grew and we found ever more ingenious arguments in order to justify our possession of this particular place, the trump card being that it was given to us by God. So we have an excuse for how we feel about people who are different from ourselves and for how we treat each other.

Our faith has spread throughout the world but we still need to learn how to live together. Ancient societies can teach us a thing or two. The indigenous peoples of southern Africa were originally easily overrun by white settlers because the idea of the ownership of land was totally unknown to them. The same was true of Native Americans who felt that they were one with the whole of creation. If that were our starting point, instead of self-preservation and possession, then we would have a foundation on which to build a much more peaceable world. These old ways, that we, from our position of superiority, have despised are in truth not primitive but civilized; they are humane. They give us a pointer as to how we might move towards what we have seen so far as an almost impossible dream, if not an unattainable vision, 'Show thyself the prince of peace; bid our jarring conflicts cease. By thy reconciling love, every stumbling-block remove'. As a hymn writer today I cannot better that sentiment.

1. Jesus, Lord, we look to thee,
   Let us in thy name agree;
   Show thyself the prince of peace;
   Bid our jarring conflicts cease.

2. By thy reconciling love,
   Every stumbling-block remove;
   Each to each unite, endear;
   Come, and spread thy banner here.

3. Make us of one heart and mind,
   Courteous, pitiful, and kind,
   Lowly, meek in thought and word,
   Altogether like our Lord.

4. Let us for each other care,
   Each the other's burden bear,
   To thy church the pattern give,
   Show how true believers live.

5. Still our fellowship increase,
   Knit us in the bond of peace:
   Join our new-born spirits, join
   Each to each, and all to thine.

6. Free from anger and from pride,
   Let us thus in God abide;
   All the depth of love express,
   All the height of holiness.

A time of mellow fruitfulness

45. Ye servants of God, your Master proclaim

I wonder what you do if you're wandering along and see a piece of litter on the pavement? Pick it up? Hygiene might make you think twice. But what about piling your dishes up in a restaurant or opening a door for another person? There's no excuse not to, unless you think that to do such things is demeaning.

Perhaps it's easier for me. I was brought up in a guest house. It was only small – mum, dad and me and a lady who used to come in on week days to help make the beds. This was back in the days of full board in Paignton in Devon. Year in and year out our visitors returned. Some came by recommendation but, for the most part, we knew them like members of the family. I can remember looking down the bookings with my parents and thinking, 'It'll be good when they come, I'll get a treat!' By the same token my parents would show by a glance, or their body language, the guests they'd rather not have. Guests could make your job easy or difficult by their consideration or lack of it.

Life's like that too. We can make life easy or tiresome for our neighbours by the tone of our voice, the little things we do or leave undone. A little thought can go a long, long way.

When I was exploring faith in my twenties it struck me that Jesus was, if nothing else, considerate. If we are to take the gifts of the Spirit seriously they are, at the very least, gifts of consideration, for 'the fruit of the Spirit is love, joy, peace, patience, kindness, generosity, faithfulness, gentleness and self-control' (Galatians 5.22–23).

Then to be like Jesus, to be inspired by Jesus' Spirit, will change our attitudes and actions in minute particulars, like picking up litter and piling up dishes, because in doing these things we make life easier for others. That brings these next words of Charles Wesley right down to earth, for we will proclaim the lordship of Jesus in our lives in as much as our lives reflect his selfless consideration.

Our actions proclaim more about us than a thousand words ever can, and Jesus went further than we are ever likely to. But we can make a start!

1. Ye servants of God, your Master proclaim,
   And publish abroad his wonderful name;
   The name all-victorious of Jesus extol;
   His kingdom is glorious, and rules over all.

2. God ruleth on high, almighty to save;
   And still he is nigh, his presence we have;
   The great congregation his triumph shall sing,
   Ascribing salvation to Jesus our king.

3. 'Salvation to God who sits on the throne!'
   Let all cry aloud, and honour the Son;
   The praises of Jesus the angels proclaim,
   Fall down on their faces, and worship the Lamb.

4. Then let us adore, and give him his right:
   All glory and power, all wisdom and might,
   All honour and blessing, with angels above,
   And thanks never-ceasing, and infinite love.

46. Give me the faith which can remove

I can remember the first sermon I ever preached, though I doubt the hearers would! At the time I was a schoolteacher and a wonderful man called Oliver Gunning – people in the Wrexham area might remember him – had me 'on note'; I was a trainee. Oliver talked to me about life, shared a love of music and taught me how to lay out my notes so that I was less likely to lose my way reading my sermon. He gave me guidance in choosing hymns and, above all, impressed me by his willingness to let me learn and make mistakes. He corrected me gently but wisely. I owe a lot to him.

Oliver had asked me to prepare a service and to preach, as I remember it, at an evening service at the English Methodist Church in Llangollen. There were Welsh-speaking churches there too. I decided to take the story of the call of Samuel and Jesus blessing the children as my Bible readings. No one I knew much bothered about the lectionary then. We sang 'Hushed was the evening hymn' and I preached. The essence of what I wanted to say, and I wouldn't change it now, is that children take things at face value and trust when adults question. It is not that the questions are unimportant; I wouldn't lecture if I thought that. It's simply that there are some things we don't need to question and others that, no matter how hard we try, we are never going to answer. Then I need

> ... Samuel's mind,
> a sweet unmurmuring faith [...]
> that I might read with childlike eyes
> truths that are hidden from the wise.

Children so often simply trust. As adults we offend them and God when we break that trust. It is that trust that we need to learn again, that 'child-like praying love', that trust of God and of each other; and we need to be worthy of that trust too.

1. Give me the faith which can remove
   And sink the mountain to a plain;
   Give me the childlike praying love,
   Which longs to build thy house again;
   Thy love, let it my heart o'erpower,
   And all my simple soul devour.

2. I would the precious time redeem,
   And longer live for this alone:
   To spend, and to be spent, for them
   Who have not yet my Saviour known;
   Fully on thee my mission prove,
   And only breathe, to breathe thy love.

3. My talents, gifts and graces, Lord,
   Into thy blessed hands receive;
   And let me live to preach thy word,
   And let me to thy glory live;
   My every sacred moment spend
   In publishing the sinners' friend.

4. Enlarge, inflame, and fill my heart
   With boundless charity divine:
   So shall I all my strength exert,
   And love them with a zeal like thine;
   And lead them to thy open side,
   The sheep for whom their Shepherd died.

47. O for a thousand tongues to sing

I remember a number of years ago a prominent Methodist making the point that though the churches in this country were in decline, worldwide Christianity and Methodism were growing. For that to be the case the followers of a Galilean carpenter needed big ideas! The Great Commission in St Matthew's Gospel speaks of all nations being disciples, learners. When John and Charles Wesley began their ministry they looked as far away as America. Initially they had little success there, but in the end the United Methodist Church became one of the largest denominations in the USA. Today Methodism has spread throughout the world. The Wesleys might have been amazed by that. But the vision was there from the start.

On 21 May 1739 Charles Wesley wrote the words of our next hymn, 'O for a thousand tongues'. The 'thousand tongues' are those who sing God's praise, having heard the good news that Christians had proclaimed. This proclamation was for everyone. Political correctness rightly questions at least two of the verses that Wesley wrote originally. 'Leap ye lame for joy' echoes Luke 4.18, but it is not the most sensitive verse ever written. Some people with disabilities are happy with this, some are not, however it is interpreted. Because something is in Scripture it is not always right for all time. We live and learn and grow in grace and, hopefully, also in sensitivity to our neighbours. The other verse would now be regarded as racist. So those we exclude. But the call is still to all nations, to all people. The call is universal as none are excluded from the compass of God's love. This is an offer for every soul.

And now a question. I wonder if you, like me, have ever done anything you regret? You've been told from the pulpit that we are forgiven by God for the things that we have done that are wrong. But the trouble is that they tend to go on hanging round us. We don't forget them and they can be like an unwanted shadow over our lives. Charles Wesley believed that God would not only forgive us but set us free from the continuing effects of the things that we've done. 'He breaks the power of cancelled sin'.

So this message that the brothers were beginning to share had the ultimate promise that those who received it might 'Anticipate [their] heaven below, and own that love is heaven'. Worth singing about indeed.

1. O for a thousand tongues to sing
   My great redeemer's praise,
   The glories of my God and king,
   The triumphs of his grace!

2. My gracious master and my God,
   Assist me to proclaim,
   To spread through all the earth abroad
   The honours of thy name.

3. Jesus – the name that charms our fears,
   That bids our sorrows cease;
   'Tis music in the sinner's ears,
   'Tis life, and health, and peace.

4. He breaks the power of cancelled sin,
   He sets the prisoner free;
   His blood can make the foulest clean,
   His blood availed for me.

5. Look unto him, ye nations, own
   Your God, ye fallen race;
   Look, and be saved through faith alone,
   Be justified by grace.

6. See all your sins on Jesus laid:
   The lamb of God was slain;
   His soul was once an offering made
   For every soul of man.

7. In Christ, our head, you then shall know,
   Shall feel, your sins forgiven,
   Anticipate your heaven below,
   And own that love is heaven.

48. Ye that do your master's will

I'm not a very keen gardener, ask my wife! She's the one with the green fingers. Gardening seems to me to be an endless chore. I love the beauty of the garden; I know to experience it someone has to make the effort. I love vegetables freshly dug from the soil, they always taste that bit better. It's just that gardening never seems to have an end. If you take it seriously you spend more time doing it than enjoying the fruits of your labours. Part of the reason for this is the way that on a freshly weeded bed new weeds appear, as if by magic, by the following morning!

There is a metaphor here for life and it's one that Charles Wesley knew well. In his sermons he pictures the life of the faithful as being continual pressing on. There is no time for rest or respite 'till we cast our crowns before thee lost in wonder love and praise'. Along the way, though we are forgiven by God, we sin again and need to be forgiven again and so the cycle continues. The fruit may come by faith but it also requires total dedication and hard work. Our lives become the gardens in which we plant and weed but rarely rest.

Perhaps it was that understanding which led to one of the best aspects of Methodism. There is, they say, nothing new under the sun. I remember a few years ago house groups became all the rage in Churches. These, we were told, would rejuvenate the Church and enable people to grow individually, spiritually and also in fellowship with each other. We had discovered what the Wesleys knew 300 years before. They called house groups 'classes'. Each class would meet regularly together. They would seek to build each other up in faith, they would take each other's spiritual temperature, confess their faults to one another, correct each other, pray for one another. There was a recognition that the high calling of the Christian was difficult, if not impossible, to achieve without the support of fellow Christians. The next hymn captures something of the essence of that ideal.

1. Ye that do your master's will,
    Meek in heart, be meeker still:
    Day by day your sins confess,
    Ye that walk in righteousness:
    Gracious souls in grace abound,
    Seek the Lord, whom ye have found.

2. Sing ye happy souls, that press
    Toward the height of holiness;
    All his promises receive,
    All the grace he hath to give;
    Follow on, nor slack your pace
    Till ye see his glorious face.

49. Come, O thou traveller unknown

Clearly, being a Christian is not easy.

St Paul had it right in the letter to the Romans when he said, 'I do not understand my own actions. For I do not do what I want, but I do the very thing I hate' (Romans 7.15). With the best will in the world all our resolutions can so easily come to nothing. We know how we should behave but it is so easy to slip up. Put simply, being good is a constant struggle. Charles Wesley brings together an image from the Old Testament and that truth to speak of the wrestling, struggling life of pilgrimage.

The story is told of Jacob wrestling with God at the Jabbok Brook (Genesis 32.24-30). Jacob is alone at night with a man. They wrestle. Jacob's hip is put out of joint; clearly he has lost the struggle. Yet he holds on and says that he will not let the man go unless he is blessed by him. At this point God, in the form of the man, names Jacob Israel.

The anonymity of the God-man comes from the unwillingness of the Jews to name God. If you call someone's name and they turn round, you have their attention. You have power over them. To know a name is to be able to exercise power. So Jacob struggles with a nameless man. But then when he seeks a blessing he is named. This is a sign that from that point forward Jacob has become God's possession, for this is not just any name but a God-given name. God has the upper hand!

The story of the struggle can be interpreted as a metaphor for the struggle of every person with God.

For Charles Wesley the name of the anonymous wrestler is revealed as 'Love'. This wrestling God of love is the 'Sun of righteousness', the healing Saviour, the one in whom the metaphorically lame can leap for joy.

111

1. Come, O thou traveller unknown,
   Whom still I hold, but cannot see!
   My company before is gone,
   And I am left alone with thee;
   With thee all night I mean to stay,
   And wrestle till the break of day.

2. I need not tell thee who I am,
   My misery and sin declare;
   Thyself hast called me by my name;
   Look on thy hands, and read it there:
   But who, I ask thee, who art thou?
   Tell me thy name, and tell me now.

3. In vain thou strugglest to get free;
   I never will unloose my hold!
   Art thou the Man that died for me?
   The secret of thy love unfold:
   Wrestling, I will not let thee go,
   Till I thy name, thy nature know.

4. Wilt thou not yet to me reveal
   Thy new, unutterable name?
   Tell me, I still beseech thee, tell;
   To know it now resolved I am:
   Wrestling, I will not let thee go,
   Till I thy name, thy nature know.

5. What though my shrinking flesh complain,
   And murmur to contend so long?
   I rise superior to my pain,
   When I am weak, then I am strong;
   And when my all of strength shall fail,
   I shall with the God-Man prevail.

6. Yield to me now; for I am weak,
   But confident in self-despair;
   Speak to my heart, in blessings speak,
   Be conquered by my instant prayer;
   Speak, or thou never hence shalt move,
   And tell me if thy name is Love.

7. 'Tis Love! 'Tis Love! thou diedst for me!
   I hear thy whisper in my heart;
   The morning breaks, the shadows flee,
   Pure, universal love thou art;
   To me, to all, thy mercies move:
   Thy nature and thy name is Love.

8. My prayer has power with God; the grace
   Unspeakable I now receive;
   Through faith I see thee face to face,
   I see thee face to face and live!
   In vain I have not wept and strove:
   Thy nature and thy name is Love.

9. I know thee, Saviour, who thou art,
   Jesus, the feeble sinner's friend;
   Nor wilt thou with the night depart,
   But stay and love me to the end;
   Thy mercies never shall remove:
   Thy nature and thy name is Love.

10. The sun of righteousness on me
    Has risen with healing in his wings;
    Withered my nature's strength, from thee
    My soul its life and succour brings;
    My help is all laid up above:
    Thy nature and thy name is Love.

11. Contented now upon my thigh
    I halt, till life's short journey end;
    All helplessness, all weakness, I
    On thee alone for strength depend;
    Nor have I power from thee to move:
    Thy nature and thy name is Love.

12. Lame as I am, I take the prey,
    Hell, earth, and sin with ease o'ercome;
    I leap for joy, pursue my way,
    And as a bounding hart fly home,
    Through all eternity to prove
    Thy nature and thy name is Love.

Changed from glory into glory

50. All glory to God in the sky

The leaves have blown from the trees and form a carpet in the local woodland. Brown, gold and russet brushed by our feet, scattered as children run to and fro, swirling in showers of colour. I love this time of year. I love the colours; I love the sight of horses, their breath misting the air. By the coast, the autumn brings high tides which can be devastating, but at the same time there is a thrill of excitement as waves crash and break on the shore. In my memory I recollect coming down from Dartmoor in my parents' car, reaching home and toasting crumpets on a real coal fire. Lovely. That glimpse of memory is comforting. But winter is waiting in the wings and is all too near.

From time to time we need to retreat out of the hurly-burly of life to something more comfortable, even if it is just to be lost for a while in the reverie of memory.

That is true in our religious lives too. It is so easy to get caught up in our imperfections and faithlessness and to worry about our inability to be as good as we might. That awareness is important but it is unhealthy if it is our only perspective. So we need to keep a firm grasp of the hope and joy which are found in the Bible. Remember that Jesus turned water into wine and that he joined a real celebration, that he spoke of God's joy being in us that our joy might be complete.

Held before the Christian is the hope that ultimately all will be well and all manner of things will be well. This is not to deny the real tragedies that come into our lives. Neither is it a counsel to allow injustice to go unchallenged until God comes to put it right. Rather it is a right counter to the doom and gloom merchants, secular and religious who would surround our lives with sadness and take away our hope. The gospel is always ultimately optimistic. That is the seed of Christmas, the essence of Easter, of resurrection, the basis of our faith.

1. All glory to God in the sky,
   And peace upon earth be restored!
   O Jesus, exalted on high,
   Appear our omnipotent Lord!
   Who, meanly in Bethlehem born,
   Didst stoop to redeem a lost race,
   Once more to thy creatures return,
   And reign in thy kingdom of grace.

2. When thou in our flesh didst appear,
   All nature acknowledged thy birth;
   Arose the acceptable year,
   And heaven was opened on earth;
   Receiving its Lord from above,
   The world was united to bless
   The giver of concord and love,
   The prince and the author of peace.

3. O wouldst thou again be made known!
   Again in thy Spirit descend,
   And set up in each of thine own
   A kingdom that never shall end.
   Thou only art able to bless,
   And make the glad nations obey,
   And bid the dire enmity cease,
   And bow the whole world to thy sway.

4. Come then to thy servants again,
   Who long thy appearing to know;
   Thy quiet and peaceable reign
   In mercy establish below;
   All sorrow before thee shall fly,
   And anger and hatred be o'er,
   And envy and malice shall die,
   And discord afflict us no more.

51. Come, let us join our friends above

On 2 November many churches observe All Souls Day or 'The Commemoration of the Faithful Departed'. In many places, there is a service to remember those who have died during the past year or even in previous years. The services take many different forms. No matter how they are conducted such acts of worship raise again questions as old as humanity: what happens when we die? There seems to be a strand in our human understanding that longs for there to be something beyond this life and to then try and picture it. The ancient Egyptians built pyramids and provided the dead with all they would need for the journey through the after-life and for their eventual destination. John the Divine, the writer of Revelation, the last book of the New Testament, imagined a new heaven and a new earth where all crying and tears would be no more. Christians have struggled with questions of judgement and the love of God. Can those who are seen as bad in the world's eyes find a way to heaven? If not, what does that say about God's love? And if they do, what of God's judgement? The Victorians pictured heaven as the perfect household, imagining chairs around an earthly hearth emptying as people died, while in heaven the family was reassembling.

Whatever model or picture we choose some things can't be challenged. Life as we know it has a beginning and an end. What happens beyond this life is beyond our experience. We only have faith, vision, inspiration and Scripture to inform us, to inspire our hope or to bolster our prejudice. For Christians there has always been an essence of hope. That hope was built around the resurrection of Jesus. There is an expectation of a better place and so Charles Wesley was able to write, 'Rejoice for a brother deceased, our loss is his infinite gain'. As St Paul wrote, 'If to live is Christ then to die is gain'. It is only a short step to singing, 'Come, let us join our friends above that have obtained the prize'.

Strange though those words may seem they are rooted in a reality of the understanding of the inevitability of death, for some 'are crossing now'. There is also a firm and very beautiful Christian hope that the dead 'on the eagle wings of love to joys celestial rise'. Poetic imagination? Perhaps. Rooted in Scripture? Certainly. Real, we know not till we die, but it is my hope, and I'd be happy for these words to be used at my funeral when the time comes.

1. Come, let us join our friends above
   That have obtained the prize,
   And on the eagle wings of love
   To joys celestial rise:
   Let all the saints terrestrial sing
   With those to glory gone;
   For all the servants of our king,
   In earth and heaven, are one.

2. One family we dwell in him,
   One church, above, beneath,
   Though now divided by the stream,
   The narrow stream of death:
   One army of the living God,
   To his command we bow;
   Part of his host have crossed the flood,
   And part are crossing now.

3. Ten thousand to their endless home
   This solemn moment fly;
   And we are to the margin come,
   And we expect to die;
   Ev'n now by faith we join our hands
   With those that went before,
   And greet the blood-besprinkled bands
   On the eternal shore.

4. Our spirits too shall quickly join,
   Like theirs with glory crowned,
   And shout to see our captain's sign,
   To hear his trumpet sound.
   O that we now might grasp our guide!
   O that the word were given!
   Come, Lord of hosts, the waves divide,
   And land us all in heaven.

52. Rejoice, the Lord is King

It is unfashionable to speak of crowns, of hierarchy, of royalty. John Wesley, or at least Methodism, it has been argued, saved the British from an equivalent of the French Revolution. Aside from the truth or otherwise of the argument, or the consequences of the outcome, the mood of the age today has become one of equality. It is offensive if someone, through an accident of birth, gets better hospital treatment than another, has a more comfortable life, a greater life expectancy. As this feeling has entered society it is only natural that we should become wary of using language of royalty in relation to God or Jesus. It is all too easy to slip from metaphor into a feeling that the words say something more about God than they were ever meant to. Then we get into the special imagery of thrones and cities, of splendour and riches and we forget the carpenter of Galilee who had nowhere to lay his head. We need to be careful.

We struggle with images which are beyond our ability to describe. How can a phrase picture the beauty of the dawn, the constancy of the tides, the eyes of a baby and a lover's kiss? How can constellations and cells, mountains and mists be understood by the merely human? We are filled with awe and stunned to silence, or we ought to be. Yet our humanity clamours for description, for explanation. We struggle to form a framework on which we can hang our images of God, our descriptions of God's nature, and we fail over and over again. Yet we go on trying. Daniel spoke of God coming out of the clouds as if on a heavenly chariot. The image was never meant to portray reality. Elijah heard God whisper on the mountainside while Isaiah met God's thunder, smoke and fire in the Temple. God comes to each generation, and each generation will try to express again what it means to meet the power behind the universe, the reality that gave birth to all reality, the God who, in human form, challenged all our norms about what it means to be a person and showed a better way.

A God of the clouds? A king reigning in triumph attended by thousands of holy people? The one who by a glance can reduce us to penitence and bring us to our knees? The one who demonstrated the length and breadth, the height and depth of love that God had for people by being willing to die at their hands rather than resist in any physical way? All of these, the reality and the pictures that try to explain it, speak of God who, when we allow it, reigns on earth.

1. Rejoice, the Lord is King.
   Your Lord and King adore;
   mortals, give thanks and sing,
   and triumph evermore:
   > *Lift up your heart, lift up your voice;*
   > *rejoice, again I say, rejoice.*

2. Jesus the Saviour, reigns,
   the God of truth and love;
   when he had purged our stains,
   he took his seat above:
   Chorus.

3. His kingdom cannot fail;
   he rules o'er earth and heaven;
   the keys of death and hell
   are to our Jesus given:
   Chorus.

4. He sits at God's right hand
   till all his foes submit,
   and bow to his command,
   and fall beneath his feet:
   Chorus.

5. Rejoice in glorious hope;
   Jesus the Judge shall come,
   and take his servants up
   to their eternal home:
   > *We soon shall hear the archangel's voice*
   > *the trump of God shall sound: Rejoice!*

Where to go next

So many hymns! If this has given you a taste for using hymns in your devotions you might like to read further. You can use your own hymn book if you like. Those who enjoy history and hymns might try to get a copy of *The Christian Year*, a collection of John Keble's texts published first in 1827. To come right up to date, Stainer & Bell have published a collection of 150 of my texts, *Reclaiming Praise*, concurrently with this book; you could look there.

Hymns in alphabetical order